A Country Without Borders
Poems and Stories of Kashmir

A Country Without Borders
Poems and Stories of Kashmir

LALITA PANDIT HOGAN

Introduction by Frederick Luis Aldama

NEW YORK
www.2leafpress.org

P.O. Box 4378
Grand Central Station
New York, New York 10163-4378
editor@2leafpress.org
www.2leafpress.org

2LEAF PRESS
is an imprint of the
Intercultural Alliance of Artists & Scholars, Inc. (IAAS),
a NY-based nonprofit 501(c)(3) organization that promotes
multicultural literature and literacy.
www.theiaas.org

Library of Congress Control Number: 2016951238
ISBN-13: 978-1-940939-57-5 (Paperback)
ISBN-13: 978-1-940939-58-2 (eBook)

10   9   8   7   6   5   4   3   2   1

Published in the United States of America

First Edition | First Printing

2LEAF PRESS trade distribution is handled by University of Chicago Press / Chicago
Distribution Center (www.press.uchicago.edu) 773.702.7010. Titles are also available for
corporate, premium, and special sales. Please direct inquiries to the UCP Sales Department,
773.702.7248.

For my parents, and for Patrick.

CONTENTS

A Note on the History of Kashmir

KASHMIR IS RENOWNED as a land of natural beauty and has often been imagined as a utopia. Four hundred years ago, Emperor Jahangir famously proclaimed of Kashmir, "If there is a paradise on earth, it is this; it is this; it is this."[1] Three centuries later, the idyllic condition of the Valley was imagined to extend to social integration as well. Thus, Mahatma Gandhi praised Kashmir for its inter-religious harmony. After the unspeakable violence of the Partition of India and Pakistan in 1947, the division of British India in which approximately one million people died in the mutual slaughter of Hindus, Muslims, and Sikhs, Gandhi commented that "in an India which had become dark all round, Kashmir was the only hope."[2] The harmonious relation of Hindus and Muslims was celebrated as a distinctive feature of "Kashmiriyat" or "Kashmiriness." The evidence for this heavenly peace was in part a matter of the literary tradition, which included a series of mystical poets who drew on both Hindu and Muslim traditions.[3]

But a little over a half-century later, Arundhati Roy could describe a murderous chaos that marks life in Kashmir. She writes, "Kashmir is a valley awash with militants, renegades, security forces, double-crossers, informers, spooks, blackmailers, extortionists, spies, both Indian and Pakistani intelligence agencies, human rights activists, NGOs, and unimaginable amounts of unaccounted-for money and weapons . . . . It's not easy to tell who is working for whom."[4] Kashmiris from the Muslim majority have few or no civil rights against the Indian military, and are also threatened by militants, both Kashmiri and foreign, often supported by Pakistan. This violence has led to perhaps 70,000 or 80,000 deaths, or more.[5] It has also led to massive incarceration, harassment, physical injury, and other harms short of death. The small Hindu minority has been almost entirely driven from their homes into exile, terrorized by prominent killings and threats from militants and their supporters. Moreover, Kashmir is a possible nuclear "flash point,"[6] making this conflict potentially dangerous to the entire globe.

What happened to change Kashmir from Jahangir's paradise on earth and Gandhi's "only hope" to this hell, "the most heavily militarized region in the world"[7] (at least in 2004)?

It is perhaps worth noting what was not the problem. Commonplaces about Hinduism emphasize caste stratification and the disabilities and cruelties that accompany such practices as untouchability. Certainly, caste restrictions have caused terrible suffering in the course of India's history. But caste is not an issue in Kashmir. The small Hindu community that remained in the Kashmir Valley in the twentieth century comprised members of the priestly caste alone—"pandits," educators and ritual practitioners by birth (though of course their actual occupations varied). There was no caste hierarchy among Kashmiri Hindus.[8]

So, what, then, was the problem? There is no explanation that is universally accepted. But there are some clear elements. In part, the picture was always too rosy. There were communal tensions and conflicts all along. ("Communalism" is the identity-based opposition of religious communities.) The anti-communalist appeals of the mystical poets make sense only in a context where communal conflict is a danger. One does not, after all, appeal to the peaceful coexistence of groups that never give a second thought to their peaceful coexistence (e.g., people who are left-handed and people who are right-handed). In Ghulam Khan's words, "Apparently the relations between the Hindus and the Muslims were very cordial and peaceful. But in fact there was a deep wave of suspicion, hostility and bitterness running at the bottom of their social relations."[9] The historical record includes Muslim rulers following "anti-Hindu policy" and Hindu rulers who confiscated mosques.[10]

The current conflict in Kashmir is only in part a matter of religious identification. It is also in part a matter of national identification, with a troubled history extending back over a century. That troubled identification was intensified in 1947, when British rule ended in colonial India.[11] Much of the Indian subcontinent was under direct British control. However, there were also semi-independent "princely states," regions where the British often controlled some aspects of governance, but recognized a non-British sovereign (even if they kept that sovereign on a short leash, so to speak). Jammu and Kashmir was one of these princely states.

The Indian independence movement had two principle components—the Congress Party and the Muslim League. The Congress Party—which included Hindus and Muslims, but was dominated by members of the Hindu community—advocated a secular democracy for all Indians. The Muslim League—which was, of course, composed primarily of Muslim South Asians—advocated a separate homeland for Muslims, thus a division between India and Pakistan. The outcome of the conflict among the British and these independence movements was the Partition of British India into Hindu-majority India and Muslim-majority Pakistan.

Part of the 1947 independence and partition was the agreement that princely states in the region would accede to either Pakistan or India. Generally, this did not pose any particular problem, as the Hindu rulers of Hindu-majority areas would accede to India, while the Muslim rulers of Muslim-majority areas would accede to Pakistan. However, the case of Kashmir—or, more precisely, the encompassing state of Jammu and Kashmir—was different. There, the maharaja was Hindu, but the majority of the population was Muslim. To make matters worse, the population included a very significant Hindu minority (principally outside the valley of Kashmir). Then there was the further complication that the main Kashmiri nationalist party, the National Conference, was not aligned with the Muslim League. The maharaja did not make a decision about accession until a Pakistan-supported uprising and invasion[12] forced him to do so. Faced with a military foe whom he could not defeat, he appealed to India and agreed to accede to India in exchange for their military aid. This entry of Jammu and Kashmir into the Republic of India was, however, qualified by promises of relative autonomy and of a plebiscite to determine the will of the people.

This first conflict between India and Pakistan resulted in a division of Kashmir, with part under Pakistani control and part under Indian control. Neither segment of Kashmir has fared particularly well since that time.[13] India never held the promised plebiscite, in part claiming that such a vote required the participation of Pakistani Kashmir. Moreover, various elements of the state's autonomy have been compromised. Indian Kashmir became increasingly militarized over the following decades, and Pakistan has supported anti-India activism in Kashmir. Polls indicate that the great majority of Indian Kashmiris and a high percentage of Pakistani Kashmiris favor independence from both Pakistan and India[14] —though the views of Hindu Kashmiris are not the same as those of the (Muslim) majority. In any case, it does not seem that the regional superpowers—India and Pakistan—are likely to allow such independence.

The current crisis can be traced to events beginning in 1987. There was extensive and widely recognized vote fraud during Jammu and Kashmir elections that year.[15] Most writers trace the rapid expansion of the anti-India militancy in Kashmir to the vote fraud.[16] That expansion may have resulted even more from the brutal treatment of the opposition activists at the time.[17] Whatever the precise reasons, the following years saw the development of an extensive insurgency with spiraling violence in which ordinary Kashmiris, both Muslim and Hindu, suffered terribly. Though there have been periods of relative calm, the situation has not been resolved, and there seems to be little hope of a resolution in the near future.[18] ▣

—Patrick Colm Hogan
University of Connecticut
Storrs, CT

NOTES

1. Cited in Ed Douglas, "Kashmir: Paradise Refound." *The Guardian* (12 March 2010). Available at http://www.guardian.co.uk/travel/2010/mar/13/kash-mir-paradise-refound-adventure (accessed 1 April 2013).

2. Quoted in P. N. K. Bamzai, *A History of Kashmir, Political, Social, Cultural: From the Earliest Times to the Present Day* (Delhi, India: Metropolitan, 1962), 669.

3. On Kashmiri Hindu and Muslim mystical poetry, see Trilokinath Raina, *A History of Kashmiri Literature* (New Delhi, India: Sahitya Academy, 2002).

4. Arundhati Roy, *Field Notes on Democracy: Listening to Grasshoppers* (Chicago: Haymarket Books, 2015), 97.

5. See Mirza Waheed, *The Collaborator* (New York: Penguin, 2011), 305, and Seema Kazi, *In Kashmir: Gender, Militarization and the Modern Nation State* (Brooklyn, NY: South End Press, 2010), xi.

6. Wajahat Habibullah, *My Kashmir: Conflict and the Prospects of Enduring Peace* (Washington, D.C.: United States Institute of Peace Press, 2008), 3.

7. Seema Kazi, *In Kashmir: Gender, Militarization and the Modern Nation State* (Brooklyn, NY: South End Press, 2010), 85

8. See, for example, T. N. Pandit, "Kashmiriyat: An Anthropological View Point," in *Kashmir and its People: Studies in the Evolution of Kashmiri Society* (New Delhi: S. B. Nangia, 2004), 183.

9. Ghulam Khan, *Freedom Movement in Kashmir: 1931-1940* (Srinagar, Kash-mir, India: Gulshan Books, 2009), 31.

10. M. J. Akbar, *Kashmir: Behind the Vale* (New Delhi, India: Viking, 1991), 53 and 69.

11. For a concise overview of Indian and Pakistani independence, see chapter 22 of Stanley Wolpert, *A New History of India*, 4th ed. (Oxford: Oxford University Press, 1993).

12. See Andrew Whitehead, *A Mission in Kashmir* (New Delhi, India: Viking, 2007), 46 and 51.

13. On human rights in Indian Kashmir, see for example "'Everyone Lives in Fear': Patterns of Impunity in Jammu and Kashmir." *Human Rights Watch* 18 (2006). On human rights in Pakistani Kashmir, see for example "'With Friends Like These . . . : Human Rights Violations in Azad Kashmir," *Human Rights Watch 18* (2006).

14. See Robert Bradnock, *Kashmir: Paths to Peace* (London: Royal Institute of International Affairs, 2010), 15, 17.

15. Šumit Ganguly, *The Crisis in Kashmir: Portents of War, Hopes of Peace* (Cambridge: Cambridge University Press, 1997), 98.

16. See, for instance, Sten Widmalm, *Kashmir in Comparative Perspective: Democracy and Violent Separatism in India* (London: RoutledgeCurzon, 2002), 77-83

17. See Habibullah (61-62) on the arrest and torture of opposition leaders.

18. For some possible routes to a peaceful resolution to the conflict, see the afterword to Patrick Colm Hogan, *Imagining Kashmir: Emplotment and Colonialism* (Lincoln, NE: University of Nebraska Press, 2016).

My Memories of Kashmir

I WROTE THE CORE POEMS included in this volume between 1996 and 1999 as an active participant in an online discussion group, "kpnet," whose membership was composed of diaspora and displaced Kashmiris, mostly Hindu Kashmiris, many of whom lost their homes during the ethnic cleansing of their community in the winter of 1990, a process that has continued thereafter. Many of their relatives, like my own, were forced to flee the valley and become refugees in Jammu, Udhampur, and other parts of India. Though my life has been interwoven with the lives of Kashmiris from all religious communities, I was born and raised in a Kashmiri Hindu family. As an ethnic group, Kashmiri Hindus are often labelled "Pandits" although not everyone's last name is "Pandit." The term "pandit" comes from Kashmir's Hindu community having been caste-less, with everyone belonging to the Brahmin caste. The caste system, as it continues to exist in India, was configured differently in Kashmir. For example, there were priests who performed rituals, and there were *karkuns* who worked in other professions and occupations but belonged to the Brahmin caste. Neither the type of work they did nor their birth-right automatically placed them in any other caste.

I grew up in Anantnag, a big city now, about twelve miles from Kulgam, our ancestral village, now a large town. In those days, we usually made the journey on a *tonga*, a horse drawn carriage, from Anantnag to Kulgam on *Shivaratri,* a spring festival celebrating the marriage of the god, Shiva, to the goddess Parvati. In this festival, nature and culture seem to come together at the end of winter, with wild flowers appearing promptly wherever ice melts and snow thins away. From my mother's room in the Kulgam house, we could see three majestic peaks of the mountains that became golden at dawn. Behind the house were rice fields, where frogs croaked, and golden rice grew rich and tasty. From a closed porch with large windows on the fourth floor, on a clear night we could see buses crossing the Banihal tunnel, which was miles away. To us, the buses appeared like glowworms. We would often count them and argue with each other about how many buses crossed over. All these villages are in South Kashmir with vast stretches of rice fields unobstructed by tall buildings, hence, this view was a wonder to us as children because none of us had any chance to travel outside of the valley. Ashmuj was a very cute, small village near Kulgam, my aunt's natal home. A beautiful stream ran through their courtyard, where women bathed in summer evenings. Amun, where my other aunt's natal home is, was on the way to Devsar, my mother's village. At one time, when I was maybe ten years old, a modern bridge, very spectacular, was built on the mountainous Veshav River, so that travel to and from became easier. Today there are buses; soon there will be trains on that route too, if they are not running already.

I went one summer to Ashmuj with my aunt and played in the pastures, along with redolent domestic animals, spooked myself with stories of imaginary creatures roaming in the cedar woods, and fabricated imaginary wild beasts not to be found in any picture book or encyclopedia. I concocted names for them, and was ridiculed by cousins and siblings. All these obscure towns and hamlets would never have become newsworthy if it were not for the insurgency. Today, news reports show bodies of militants or soldiers sprawled on the streets or on the slopes of hills, wearing hand-knit sweaters soaked in blood. A young soldier from some small town in Uttar Pradesh, or Maharashtra, or Rajasthan, or some other Indian province, dead like stone, leaving behind a grieving mother, perhaps his betrothed: some shy young girl. This spectacle is unsettling, though I take a measure of interest in the place names having become known, appearing in major Indian newspapers, like *The Hindu* and *Indian Express.* I wish the places had become known for being pretty villages where good life was once lived.

Still, at the end of a full day of grading papers and attending meetings, I find myself doing a Google search, not to seek news, but to seek connection. Khannabal, about ten miles from Kulgam and two miles from Anantnag, also figures prominently in this kind of violent news. As I read this, I am reminded that my college was in Khannabal, which brings up good memories. It had an exceptionally good library, and the grounds boasted beautiful flowers tended with dedication by a kind old man. I remember his wrinkled face, flushed by the sun, and wish I had learnt from him the obscure Kashmiri names of many varieties of roses that he took pride in.

My memories are of a primarily rural, agricultural Kashmir. In contrast, the news stories are not only of an urbanized Kashmir but also of a covert battlefield. Urbanization, such as the train tracks, and beautifully laid out train stations all over Kashmir now, including Khannabal, seeks some type of progress, some type of common good. The shock to my sensibility does not come from the disappearance of an idealized pastoral; it comes from how it has been replaced by unplanned, haphazard urbanization that makes what was once beautiful, decidedly ugly. Inhospitable. Environmental degeneration that urbanization can sometimes bring (when it is not well thought out) is a shock to the ecosystem. As a necessary consequence of industrial and post-industrial development, this shock has, indeed, come to many places in the world, and has been written about. In Kashmir, however, urbanization is intensified by consanguinity with hyper-militarization and war.

In addition to the generalized atmosphere of violence and instability that seems to have become the new norm since 1990, the trigger for my memories was the burning down of our ancestral house in Kulgam, Kashmir. Built by our grandfather it was more than a house to our family; it was a living memory of our ancestors, including my grandparents who lived and died in this place. The erasure of that house from the face of Kashmir's earth took me immediately to the spot where my grandmother died. Because the river was a bit too far for her to walk to, she collapsed while performing sun-salutations at a public water tap. The tap was nestled between two cedar trees, on a slope, which caught the morning sun in a delightful way. My grandmother had to break her fast of nine days, a fast that heads of families used to observe during Navaratri (nine days of the goddess celebrated throughout India). She did not regain consciousness, and remained in a coma for three days. Because of old age, she was exempted from such a rigorous fast, but she insisted. Hers was a good death, I say to myself. She died just outside the home her husband built, where many of her grandchildren grew up, where many weddings and childbirths occurred, where her six daughters-in-law grew up from shy village brides to mothers and grandmothers. My grandmother was a delicate, slight woman; our loving neighbor cradled her in his arms and brought her home. In contrast, during the 1990s and thereafter, many of Kashmir's old people, as precious as my grandmother, died bad deaths in refugee camps outside of Kashmir: lonely, harried, bedraggled and dispossessed. In the Kashmir valley, many grandmothers like her, from the Muslim community, must have died with bitter thoughts lingering in their brains: of dead, disappeared grandsons. Some of these women, I feel sure, died looking out the window at the house of their (Hindu) female friend, burnt to cinders, gathering moss.

In the early 1990s, our house in Kulgam was occupied by a group of militants who did not speak Kashmiri. Later, it was empty for some time, and then it was burnt down, floor by floor. It was not random arson, but a deliberate act in which the local government clearly participated. The first flash of this news came to me in a very peculiar way, a tiny sentence in a letter from my father, scribbled at the edges of an aerogramme, as postscript. My father, who died on September 7, 2007, would never mention the house again. It was a significant loss to him. What impelled him to maintain a stunned silence about such a great loss is a mystery that I do, somehow, understand. Oblivion can be healing and a way to move forward. It is a kind of forgiveness my father was capable of. For some of us, ghosts of memory persist and cannot be put to rest. The fiction and poetry collected in this volume represent a measure of how I chose to deal with the loss, and the trauma.

What happened to all the books that were in the house? I would wake up in the middle of the night, asking this question and wonder about my uncle's law books, my father's books, mostly in Sanskrit and most on Kashmir Shaivism, and my grandfather's Persian classics. The house, a humble four-floor home, had an attic made of cedar wood that children of a certain age would've easily exchanged for a pair of loving parents. The outer walls of indented colored brick, impeccable masonry, artful woodwork on window panes and balconies with inner walls of mud (not cement). It was a secure shelter from rain, frost and ice, a good, solid habitation. What common good was achieved by burning it down?

What happened to our things? Were they burnt down? Had they been looted? No one knows. Or, if anyone knows, they are not willing to talk about it. Of course, houses have things in them belonging to the people who lived there. When houses are illegally occupied, the occupier is the master, and when they are destroyed (in this case, burnt down), it's done to deter a return of its owners: their accumulated memories turned to smoke. It is also done to shame, humiliate and intimidate the owners, indigenous inhabitants of the valley. Today, Kulgam's District Police Office (DSP) building stands where our house was. It is ironic.

The second important trigger, tied to the destruction of our house is my associations with place names in Kashmir, how they conflict with stories of violent encounters between the army and the militants. The names of towns, villages, rivers, springs, lakes, mountains and hills that are evocative of much that is treasured in my memory, have now become indelibly tied to internecine violence. It is as if memory itself is endangered, susceptible to violation, if not rescued and preserved. Veshav is the river my mother crossed (being ferried by a horse) when I was ten days old, and I fell from her lap into the river. I was saved, obviously, to tell the story. On that day mother was going to Devsar, across the river, to be at her father's funeral. He died tragically at a young age. As it turns out they had cremated him already, not expecting a daughter who had recently given birth to make the journey, although she was only a few miles away. My Kulgam grandfather chose not to hide bad news from my mother as he may have been expected to. He arranged for her to be taken to Devsar. Unfortunately, the Devsar folks did not wait for her. Such conflicts emerging from cultural differences between tiny hamlets (barely five miles apart) are amusing to me today and make me smile, though in this case, not having a final sight of her father's body traumatized my mother. One afternoon three weeks before she died on January 11, 2008, my laconic mother remembered her natal home. "In sunny afternoons like this," she mused, "but with a great deal of snow on the ground, in our Devsar home, a host of crows used to come down the hill into our courtyard and I used to feed them rice puffs." I realized with a shock that after the summer of 1988, she never visited Devsar again, never visited Kashmir again. Her only homage to that home was this cryptic memory of crows making raucous noise, waiting to be fed.

This is the immediate context, but the poems gathered here capture what is, sadly, not uncommon in today's globalized world, many parts of which are excessively militarized. The human cost of the high premium placed on war and on militant revolutions, as well as counter revolutions, is massive. It has given rise to a great deal of anguish and affliction, and has created a generation of displaced persons and refugees. Kashmir, as I know it, has borne a very large portion of this massive human cost.

The Making of A Country Without Borders

BEFORE 1990, HINDUS WERE a minority in Kashmir that was large enough to show in demographic maps. Their forced migration in 1990 cleansed the Kashmir valley of Hindus; now there are only a few thousand left. This is part of the sociological context in which kpnet in the 1990s served to bring a fragmented and exiled community together. As it happens in such communities, the political and ideological discussions sometimes became difficult and created dissension. At first I participated in political discussions but later I decided instead to write and share poems, as I had been writing poems and stories for many years. A significant portion of the kpnet membership, as it existed then, read and reacted positively to the poems. Their words of praise for the artistry of my poems, and a shared sense of loss of history, home, heritage and culture holds great value for me.

Eventually, I was asked to publish the poems on the Kashmir Overseas Association's (KOA) website. I and Sunil Fotedar, who was director of the website and proved to be a great editor for me, selected twenty-three poems to publish as a book on the KOA's official website. Around the same time, I was given a recognition award for service to Kashmiri culture through my poetry. Later, Kashmir News Network (KNN) prepared and published a very nicely put together online volume of *Sukeshi Has a Dream and Other Poems of Kashmir*. As we live in a digital age today, the poems were read widely and globally. A poet from Pakistan, Muhammad Yamin, translated some poems, including "Autumn-Song: Kartik Posh" (p. 111) into Urdu, and published them in a premier Pakistani journal, *Symbol*. Students from Kashmir University have, from time to time, requested to publish some of the poems in local magazines, and have wanted to refer to the poems in their research. Biju Raj Kochi, a journalist, interviewed me for the Kerala newspaper, *Mathrubhumi*, and later translated, "Father" (p. 29) to Malayalam. The story "Family and Friends" (p. 5) along with several other poems was published on another literary and cultural online outlet, *Indereunion* (www.indereunion.net) that included a long interview with me, which the editor translated to French.

In terms of style, the poems are obviously written in free verse, in the manner of mid-twentieth century American poetry, especially the affective poetics of the Confessional Poets. Sylvia Plath comes to mind. William Carlos Williams also comes to mind. William Blake, whose poetry I learned to love when I was a school child in Kashmir remains an unattainable ideal, but what he taught me was clarity of vision, and why some degree of poetic madness is necessary. Other connections of this sort can be made; the poetics, however, has something pan-Asian to it, particularly Indian and Japanese.

I wrote the majority of these poems while I was, in my scholarship, working on Comparative Aesthetics. At the same time, I designed and taught a new course on International Literature, and would explain these poetic concepts to students. Some of that work melded unconsciously with the architectonics of poetic metaphor deployed in these poems. Coincidently, the foundational theorists of the Rasadhvani Poetics of India were Kashmiris. I was co-editor and contributing author to a pioneering work on non-European traditions in literary and poetic theory, and this work coincided with my writing the poems included in this volume. A major portion of this poetic theory developed in the writings of Kashmir's Sanskrit writers, Anandavardhana, Bhattanayaka, and Abhinvagupta, who are all discussed in my long essay on rasadhvani poetics.[1] Bhattanayaka's writings are only indirectly referred to, but Anandavardhana's and Abhinavagupta's writings are preserved, translated and discussed widely today by Indian and non-Indian writers.

The term *rasa,* in Sanskrit (as I use it), refers to art emotion, what the reader or spectator feels. *Dhvani* literally means echo. It is a term postulating a concept that poetic meaning cannot be paraphrased because it functions through indirection, or the echoing effect. A relatively banal example of it is innuendo; at higher levels of cognition and affect associated with poetry, the idea is that poetic meaning should be a product of resonance, that is, of *dhvani.* This presupposes a gap between literal statement and suggestion, and poetic meaning reverberates in that in-between space. ("Reverberation" is a favorite phrase for the Sanskrit theorists.) For example, my poem, "Seasons" (p. 47) is not about seasons, although seasonal change in Kashmir is beautiful, since the valley (unlike our Wisconsin) had six distinct seasons before global warming and unpredictable weather patterns began to impact the typology of seasons. The poem investigates how life events, marked inevitably by violence, clash with a life regulated by seasonal change. As I am penning this preface, we have had news of violence all around us in the middle of a bountiful and beautiful Midwest summer. Although our chaos here does not compare with the uncontained chaos in Kashmir, in this case the meaning of "seasons" extends as easily to seasons of politically motivated violence, which clash with the ripening, blossoming and greening of nature.

A more important aspect of the rasadhvani poetics for this volume is the role played by emotion and affect. A foundational presumption of this theory is that each work of art should be, or always is, organized by one emotion, while other emotional states, moods, and so forth, play ancillary, circulatory and reinforcing roles. Thus, one might think of the role that humor, and the early desultory lightheartedness plays in *Romeo and Juliet* that reinforces pathos and tragedy. Similarly, the emotional handcuff of hate (as today's emotion theorists would label it) that the two rival families are locked into encounters its unlocking antithesis: the love of Romeo and Juliet. No matter how ill-advised and narcissistic this suicidal teenage love might seem today to some readers, it is ultimately sacrificial, challenging social and familial imperative of hate: *the ancient grudge.* In a lyric poem, things will work out differently; the speaking subject, the lyric "I" will be a narrator as well as an experiencing, observing consciousness.

Spreading the qualia of affect—and also the re-gathering of echoes around a point (as it happens in music)—is the affective poetics that I hope the poems in this volume achieve. In addition to the poetics of rasadhvani (Kashmiri in origin), the Japanese concept of "unity" of an artwork, or a tea ceremony as ritual, also plays a part, although unconsciously. This unity is signified by the principle of jo-ha-kyu, as Zeami develops it in the context of dramatic structure of the Noh play (breaking open, climaxing, and quickening to the finale). [2] This concept does not envision unity as the strict Aristotelian beginning, middle and end. *Jo* is more like the *alaap* in a classical Indian musical composition, the raga. *Kyu* is like *jhala* at the end of a *raga*. Ha can be likened to alternating units of *drut* (fast) and *vilambit*

(slow, drawn out), the tempos in the middle of a raga, or the alterna-
tions between *aaroha* (rising) and *avaroha* (falling) of notes.

While writing these poems, I continually listened to Indian classi-
cal music, both instrumental and vocal. D. V. Paluskar's *Raga Shree*
audiotape had to be replaced several times because I listened to it
incessantly. Paluskar is the legendary Indian musician (vocalist) from
Maharashtra who died young, and the *Raga Shree* performance was
his swan song.

The poems, "The Yellow River" (p. 27) and "Seasons" exemplify
the *jo-ha-kyu* structure, while the rise and fall of notes, slow and
fast movements of the classical Indian raga, can be sensed in all
the poems, and even the stories. *Rasadhvani* aesthetics, though
extended to verbal arts in theory and practical criticism over centu-
ries, developed first in connection with the performance arts such
as music and drama, and it is essentially an affective poetics. Per-
haps of equal importance when contemplating these poems is the
Japanese concept of *sabi*. A sense of *sabi,* as it appears in many
instances in *A Country Without Borders,* is defined by Basho as
"loneliness," not just loneliness of people, but "the loneliness of all
things portrayed in a poem."[3]

Sabi is also associated with objects (in ceramics and high art) that
show age and the impact (even ravages) of time, and is the opposite
of flashy, smooth, new looking objects of art, or home furnishings.
In my view, it is an aesthetic of abjection, loneliness, concretely
depicted in poetry (and art) in represented objects and persons that
have encountered time and history: the wear and tear, and damage,
which according to Japanese theorists, makes them evocative. It is
a kind of poetry that exists already in nature, in homes, city design,
pottery, variety of objects and habitations: plant, animal and human.
A prime example from this volume is Gafar's house (in "Family and
Friends"), and the few remaining objects belonging to his dead wife
and friend that he gathers together as remembrances, and ties them
up as a bundle in Amina's bridal scarf. The broken-down temples
everywhere in Kashmir, mentioned in several poems, or burnt down
houses, as well as tattered clothes and house fronts, dysfunctional

fountains in the gardens, such as in Sherbag in Anantnag, mentioned in the poem, "Azadi: 1989-1995" (p. 23) evoke a sense of *sabi*. The decrepitude and loneliness suggests a mute rebellion, or resistance to being forgotten and belittled.

This brings us to the opposite concept of *yugen*, which was very important to Zeami (1644-1694), whose Noh plays, *Atsumori,* and others, I taught in my international literature class consistently from 1996 to 2006. *Yugen,* as defined by Zeami, is the majesty and mystery of things. It is a little like the sublime in *Longinus.* In Japanese art, a cherry tree in full bloom is an emblem for *yugen*. Coincidentally, a cherry tree in full bloom in Kashmiri life is still, even in these bad times, seen to hold some secret, some mystery, beauty and majesty, much like the concept of *yugen*. These cross-cultural parallels, in the first place, attracted me to Japanese literature. However, what is common across cultures is often elaborated, exalted and embellished through specific myths, rites, rituals and symbols unique to each culture.

Many poems in *A Country Without Borders* refer to the mystery and majesty of the gods that my Kashmiri upbringing etched in my memory through very elaborately performed rituals. Apart from questions of belief and faith, these rituals, especially as they were performed in our home by my father with patience and precision, had something of *yugen* in them, as does the majestic beauty of the Pir Panjal range, and the Himalayas, which is at times celebrated in the poems. In "Sukeshi Has a Dream" (p. 67), the dream vision of the goddess that the child Sukeshi has, that fleeting moment may be thought to encode *yugen*. In the heart of loneliness, evoked by *sabi,* is the mystery and majesty of *yugen*.

Another example from this volume would be narrative captured through the focalization of an apotheosis of some sort. Towards the end of the story, "Forest Dweller" (p. 115), from the father's perspective, the child, Mridu's ascension is described thus: "They become taller, reach the sky. They raise her up. Mridu's laughter turns into a whine, then terror, but she does not fall. She vanishes into the night sky" (p. 116). What I was thinking at the time was the story of Lord

Krishna's birth in captivity. As soon as the news of Krishna's birth reaches the king, the prison is stormed by his guards. Krishna's twin sister is killed by being smashed to the ground, while the infant Krishna, being an *avatara* of Vishnu, one of the gods of the Trinity, is miraculously saved. Her body, however, does not suffer the indignity of female infanticide; instead she is changed to lightning. There is something in this, like the transformations that are told in Ovid's *Metamorphoses*. Long before I read Ovid, as children we were told this other story—that, when lightning appears in the skies it is a reenactment (in nature) of the crime against Lord Krishna's twin sister. In effect, through this story we were taught about tyranny, about sacrifice, about transformation and regeneration. Even as a child I was skeptical about the story as fact, yet in some small way it conveyed the idea of mystery, of epiphany, of poetry that makes sense when life does not. Over time, this story of lightning that my mother never tired of telling, became larger than fact, truer than history. It is, after all poetry and story that, across all cultures, captures patterns of human experience.

Even though the majority of the texts collected in this volume are poems, I also include several prose narratives. "Family and Friends" is a tale that distills my own experience of Kashmir's destruction, my encounters with suffering, mourning family and friends, and all sorts of news reports, rarely good, mostly bad and ugly. As a repository of this experience, I identify with the two main characters, Gafar and Neelesh. Even though Gafar is the protagonist, and Neelesh is just there, he is as important. They are, as their names indicate, Hindu (Neelesh) and Muslim (Gafar). Safaya is a typical Hindu last name; Dar is a typical Muslim last name (though a variant, Dhar, is typically a Hindu last name). When writing of Kashmir's violent history, people set up an idealized notion of a golden age of Kashmir, which never really existed. Tensions and conflicts were always there, a staple of life. However, outside of those conflicts there was everyday life, where the relationships between Hindus and Muslims as friends, neighbors and people who did business with each other, were based on trust, friendship, and loyalty.

Diversity is essential to the formation of a pluralistic community. Much of the ethos of reciprocity and trust that received a rude shock in the winter of 1990, and afterwards, has stayed alive in the minds and memories of a certain age-group among Kashmiris. The rise of militancy changed the scenario dramatically; the timeless bond of love and trust between the two communities received a horrific jolt. Hindus and Muslims were suddenly confronted with grave threats from various quarters and both groups began to harbor suspicion. With the death of older age groups, what will remain is hard to tell.

Aside from the question of what will happen to human relations and political structures, and how competing interests of the many stakeholders in Kashmir will configure themselves, *A Country Without Borders* is poetry and fiction of exile that is not bound to Kashmir alone. The protagonists of the story, "Family and Friends," are likewise not bound to Kashmir alone, but represent people who are neglected, left out of history and history writing, because they are not perceived as stakeholders in the political game that is played out in their region, in their habitat. However, they are stakeholders in imaginative reconstructions of their anguish and misery. This stakeholder-ship of subjects and subject positions crosses boundaries and borders between India and Pakistan, Indian Kashmir and Pakistani Kashmir: this is the country in the cultural *imaginary,* that must remain *without borders, without walls.*

Through imagination we can commemorate people like Amina, her sons, and Neelesh, those who perished, Siddharth who lost his childhood home, his father, and his friend, and Gafar, who lives on to mourn all, but has become silent and silenced. In doing so, we can pay homage to the long tradition of anti-communalist Kashmiri writing, such as the writing of Lalleshvari: the foundational Kashmiri poet of the fourteenth century. By recuperating a loss through a new kind of poetics that is rooted in ancient India, Europe, America, Asia, an aesthetics that joins what is separated by the nefarious agency of weapons, cultural hegemony, and material power, this new poetic idiom will celebrate the earth and its denizens. Through this medium we can simultaneously mourn the loss of a beloved habitat, as we celebrate what emerges out of anguish and suffering: transformation, not annihilation. ▣

—Lalita Pandit Hogan
University of Wisconsin
LaCrosse, WI
July 5, 2016

NOTES

1. "Dhvani and 'The Full Word': Suggestion and Signification from Abhinavagupta to Jacques Lacan." *College Literature* 23.1 (Feb. 1996): 142-164. Special issue on "Comparative Poetics: Non-Western Traditions in Literary Theory," edited by Patrick Colm Hogan and Lalita Pandit.

2. Mae J. Smetburst, "The Appeal of a Plotless Tragedy," in "Comparative Poetics: Non-Western Traditions in Literary Theory," eds. Patrick Colm Hogan and Lalita Pandit, Special Issue, *College Literature* 32.1 (Feb 1996): 67-80. In her discussion, Mae Smetburst argues that Aeschylus's tragedy is less Aristotelian, more in keeping with the *jo-kyu-ha* structure.

3. Lalita Pandit, "Afterword: Non-Western Literary Theories and What to Do With Them," in *Comparative Poetics: Non-Western Traditions of Literary Theory, Special Issue, College Literature 23:1* (Feb. 1996): 182.

INTRODUCTION

Winged Flights of Tellurian Sublimity

LIKE A DREAM WEAVER, a Rishi or poet-as-seer, Lalita spins verse and prose lines that open us to new repositories of remembrance from birth to death—and life in death. Her words breathe life into the world anew, and in very unexpected ways. They lift us from the ashes of a world filled with fear, greed, and tyranny.

Lalita's carefully sculpted poetry and prose ask: what do we make of our intrinsic connection—where our mind and body enter and then grow in the world—to our place of birth, our "natal" place, our nation when it has been ripped from underneath us? What does it mean to exist in-between places? What does it mean to be of no place? Lalita as demiurge, let's listen to some of the many of her resplendent creations.

In "My Father's Country" her poet-voice drops us into the northern region of India known as Kashmir, ferrying us through a labyrinthine multispace filled with suffering, violence and repression; an unnatural place where moonlight "unreports deaths" and "embers blaze blue inside"; a place filled with ghosts of those murdered and exiled; a space, too, where life anxiously awaits. In a formidable leap of imagination and great poetic skill and risk, here, too Lalita conjoins the Trojan War, the ancient Greek religious narratives and family tragedies and Homer's poems with the tragic history of Kashmir and its grief-stricken families forced into exile or annihilation. In "Azadi: 1989-1995" Lalita creates a poet-voice absent of futile yearning, inspired by millenarian struggle, and infused of the Promethean labor and aspiration. A voice clamoring for a freedom that cannot be quenched until equality, fraternity, independence, true self-rule and economic, political, and cultural democracy are attained. In "The Yellow River" Lalita invents a restless poet-voice that dips our minds into a universe where everything flows, as Heraclitus declared. A flow also not unlike the dreary Acheron and Styx, but now filled to the brim by the waste criminally discharged by capitalist greed and barbarism. In "Father" Lalita creates a poet-voice of war that moves within the penumbra of our worst, most unbearable nightmares, where tortured children appear as broken packages on our door-steps. In "Summer Rain" we feel the deep tug between the renewal of life with July rains in Wisconsin and in Kashmir, and the failure to do so with a mother's tears.

Extending the line of great poets from yogi (Lala Ded) and free-dom-fighter poets (Mahadevi Varma and Sarojini Naidu), Lalita's exquisitely spun, inter-connected concentric web of poems operate on multiple levels that ask that we reorganize fundamental parts of our inner selves.

They ask that we read them in English, but feel them as made of the thoughts and feelings of an underlying Kashmiri, Sanskrit, or Hindi linguistic experience. They ask us to establish connections between objects and subjects that often are very distant in time, in space, in memory and recollection, cognition and affective tone. They ask us to slide from one concentric circle to another as she intertwines tropes, metaphors, and analogies from different cultural traditions. They ask that we feel, think, and remember in ways that may summon a virtuous worldview—one I so cherish but that has lain dormant and fatigued for an eternity. They ask that we wake once again to the intensity of thought and feeling of the past and present as one.

In his *Nicomachean Ethics* and in his *Metaphysics*, Aristotle talks about all human activity as purposeful or goal oriented. He gives the example of the carpenter building the table. The carpenter has an idea and then turns this idea into an object that corresponds to the idea. Lalita is a carpenter who knows well her craft and tools; she knows well how to cut, shave, notch, and glue together sound and word patterns, syllables and phrases, stress and alliteration, caesurae and breaks and bridges, rhymes and rhythms to sculpt her raw material (the infinite facets of reality) into something wondrous and new. She is a maker of artifacts that immerse us into the life of her various Kashmiri subjects in ways that the most distant readers are inclined to find accurate and relevant.

Lalita is the maker of spatially designed, purposefully segmented visual/aural artifacts we call poetry, endowed with that power to steer our imagination, our emotions, our thoughts, and our perceptions toward both the outside world and our intimate experiences in ways we will not easily forget. Each of her poems gracefully and resoundingly remind us that while the verbal in poetry is a craft, it is also a sensibility, a direction and a set of indirections, a plenitude of meaning and reference and an intriguing void, a gap to be filled, enigmatic suggestions, and many hints for the reader and listener to achieve understanding and pleasure and awe by becoming a co-creator. Finally, in her mastery of direction and indirection, Lalita winds us in and through Kashmir's histories of struggle, darkness, and despair to bring us into a space of light and life. ▣

—Frederick Luis Aldama
Arts & Humanities Distinguished Professor
Ohio State University
Columbus, OH

Family and Friends

GAFAR IS SOORTRAG'S BEST BAKER. He bakes a variety of breads, like salt bread with fennel and sesame seeds, and sweet bread with almonds. The most important thing for him is to bake an abundance of plain bread, *lavasah,* thin loaves of bread that reflect light. During his father's time one could buy twenty-four loaves with one rupee. His favorite customers got extra loaves thrown in. My friend's mother got bread almost for free.

When they were young, Gafar's father, Ramzan Dar, wanted to marry my friend's mother, Fatima. She did not like him because he had a beard. She thought only grandfathers, Mullahs, and Sufi Fakirs, are entitled to beards. My mother was also a follower of Ahad Juv, a Sufi Fakir much revered in the community, a large cluster of towns and villages in South Kashmir. I remember two things about Ahad Juv: (1) the sweet tea, made in a big samovar in his hut, was the tastiest; and (2) when he said to my mother, "this girl of yours will get a *vazifa* (scholarship); send her to school." He also told her my father's fainting fits would go away on their own in a few years, and they did. It seems in her youth, my mother's close friend, Fatima refused Ramzan Dar, but now in her old age, she is worried about Gafar. Mother says for Fatima, Gafar is like her own son.

The house above Gafar's bakery was built during his grandfather's time. When Gafar was still alive, the line of shops attached to the house formed a market. The grocery was owned and run by Abdul Khalik Dar, Gafar's father's older brother, and the one next to it was rented by a cloth merchant, Dina Nath Gurutu. The youngest of Gafar's uncles had his butcher shop neck to neck with Gurutu's colorful store, and the milkman, green grocer, and chemist were in the back. Safaya Brothers' General Merchandise Store was also in the back. The police building is still where it was then, right in front, across the street.

None of the shops are in use now, except for Gafar's bakery. Of the sons, only he stayed on. All of his cousins went to college and moved on to Kashmir University, Aligarh Muslim University, and other faraway places. Many of the Gurutu and Safaya kids who went to study outside of Kashmir never came back. It was a gradual exodus of Kashmiri Hindus, but we did not see it that way back then. All Gafar's cousins who went away for studies did return to Kashmir, and some of them now live in Srinagar. One is a lawyer there, and another is a professor of Persian at the university.

Gafar's brothers live in a town near Soortrag, but the house on Zahar Street in Soortrag is still considered common property. Gafar occupies one portion of this sprawling house, while the rest of it is in a state of disrepair. At one time, not long ago, his sons lived in the upstairs rooms of their part of the house. Gafar and his wife, while taking secret delight in their children, used to complain about their youthful wildness, the noise they made, and the way they thundered down the stairs. As the boys became more mature, there was still the rough play and peals of laughter, but there was also something else –secret, serious meetings that were conducted behind closed doors.

Amina took note of the fact that Mushtaq's closest friend, Siddharth Safaya, was never invited to these meetings. In fact, once he stopped by to ask for Mushtaq, and when Amina ran upstairs to tell her son, he quickly opened the door, body blocking her view of, and access to, the room. She had never seen him like that. Amina told Siddharth the truth. Mushtaq was home; there was a meeting going on and he could not go out with Siddhu. However, she did not tell him the whole truth.

At the top of the stairs, Mushtaq had whispered in her ear: "Tell Siddhu never to come here again. Tell him to stay as far away as he can."

Amina did not have the heart to tell him that. Siddhu kept coming to the house to ask for Mushtaq. Each time he looked sadder than before, until he went away, in November 1988, to live with his grandparents in Jammu.

For several years the rooms were repeatedly searched: by the police, the army and the insurgents. After the sound and fury of the searches ended, Gafar and Amina did not want to go upstairs. It was as if the second floor of the house had become forbidden territory, cut off from the rest of the house. They never fully comprehended what had been found there, what had been hidden, and by whom. Once, the police found two non-Kashmiri speaking fugitives in the attic. They had been hiding there for several days. Amina did not know. Perhaps Gafar knew. Perhaps one of her sons knew. When such things happened, one begins to doubt one's closest kin. The right hand no longer knows what the left hand has done.

One October morning, in one of those awful years, Gafar and Amina buried Akhtar. He was the youngest and he died first. Red leaves of Chinar, lifted by the breeze, fell into his grave. There were no flowers, no mourners. The twins, Shakil and Rashid, died a year later, in Pulwama. Their funeral was a public affair. Mushtaq was there. He had identified the bodies. Shakil and Rashid took on false names for reason of subterfuge. Amina argued that since the names were not theirs, maybe the bodies were not theirs either. How can anyone identify a son, a brother, a lover, a husband, in a bloodied corpse? Gafar and Amina never went to the *Shaheed Mazaar* in Srinagar, to visit the graves.

Akhtar's story was different. He was killed for being an informer. A lot of money was taken from the treasury in Kulgam. Many arrests were made; some of the money was recovered. Akhtar may have informed about some who were involved. They had killed many people in Kulgam the day of the robbery and had burnt a Hindu home. Akhtar had been part of that group, but had later defected. A month later, they found him in Ashmuj and killed him. Mushtaq brought the body home. Soon enough rumors started about Mushtaq as well. Gafar and Amina waited, no longer able to feel or think a thing. In a sort of stupor they waited. Eventually, a note was delivered in the middle of the night.

The note said, "Mushtaq has been killed. I buried him. I am his friend." Nothing more was ever known. The messenger was muffled; there was no way to know who he was.

There was a letter in Mushtaq's shirt pocket, addressed to some girl who studied at the Anantnag Women's College. The letter was filled with quotations from Nizami's *Laila and Majnun.* In between, there were quotations in English. Alfred Lord Tennyson's "It is better to have loved and lost/Than never to have loved at all." There was no date on it, but the letter was surely written by Mushtaq. It was hard to tell if the sender meant to hand-deliver it, or mail it. Mushtaq's loss was the hardest for Amina. She took to her bed a month after the mysterious stranger's visit. Nine months later, she died.

Once the final mourning period was over, Gafar realized how much had been taken away from him. Caring for his wife in her last days was a trial. Amina was a difficult patient. In her pain and confusion, she blamed Gafar for their ill fortunes. She cursed him for his lack of ambition, and for the thwarted ambitions of their sons. She blamed him for being too stupid to stay in the bakery business. She said it was because of him that their sons wandered away to distant parts of the valley. To her all the southern towns and hamlets –Kulgam, Ashmuj, Khannabal, and Anantnag—were too distant, too alien.

For several nights after the funeral, Gafar slept soundly. His health improved. A peace seemed to settle on the house, the shop and the street. In mid-July of that year, the river flooded. There was hardly any damage. Floodwaters receded in the same quiet way in which they had overstepped the land. Like everyone else, Gafar remained housebound for three whole days. The silence got to him. It became a voice and it said, "They died and you live. *Tim mokliyi sarriye ch' chukh zinda, haenya masheed hund Jinn hyuve* (their lives ended; you are alive like the Jinn of the no-longer used, or uninhabited, mosque)." The echoing of these words, night and day, maddened him. He tore up his hair, struck his head against the wall, and bruised his face with his nails. After the floodwaters had fully abated, his brothers came to see him and took him to the trauma center of the local hospital. After a few days of incessant weeping, heavy medication, and ministrations of the nurses, another kind of calm descended on Gafar. He stopped talking. For five years now, he has remained silent like death. Although nothing was wrong with his speech organs or brain, Gafar could not be persuaded to use human speech, even to answer the simplest, the most necessary questions.

When his wife was alive, and after the deaths of his sons, Gafar would wake up in the middle if the night to pray, hoping that one day in the merciful world of Allah, he will behold their faces. His business did extraordinarily well in those days. Out of sympathy, people came to him in throngs. When his wife died and he stopped talking, people became suspicious. They thought he was mad and they considered madness contagious. They stopped buying his bread. Some thought Gafar had finally lost faith in the mercy of Allah.

As far as Gafar is concerned, the one constant in his life is his work. He continues to bake bread as before, selling it to the occasional customer. Every afternoon, he packs a huge pile of paper-thin bread in a sack. Carrying this load, the baker walks all the way to the riverfront where once there were five temples. Ten miles from where she emerges from Wular Lake, Vitasta looks like an ocean at this point. One can barely see the other shore. At the embankment above the stone steps, Gafar can be seen seated on a mount. The catalpa and the four chinar trees are still there, undisturbed by history—so, it seems, is Gafar as he cuts each moonlike bread into twenty-four pieces. The birds have become used to this method. They wait, trusting that each will get its share.

Last year, Gafar tried to kill himself. At the end of a long day, when the waters were particularly high, he just sat there—allowing the darkness to make him indistinguishable from the ruins of a temple, trees and the river. As he was about to jump, it felt like someone gently touched his shoulder. He could not see. There was no one there, but surely someone had stopped him. Not only that, he felt a presence near him, a man, taller than him. For the first time since the deaths, Gafar felt he was not alone. Someone was near him, though he could not see who it was. He stretched out his hand; there was no garment to take hold of. Still, the feeling of someone being near was true, as true as the news of each death. Gafar was too overcome to speak, though he, for once, felt the need and inclination to speak. After a few moments, he felt whoever it was had moved away. Gafar ran after until he reached home, but no one was there.

Of his family and friends, Dr. Safaya and Amina were the only two deaths Gafar witnessed. A few months after Siddharth left, Dr. Safaya sent the rest of the family to Jammu. He stayed on alone, guarding the ancestral house in which several of the Safaya families used to live in separate quarters. At different times, all fled to Jammu or Udhampur. Only Neelesh remained. At the hospital, the doctor in him attended to wounded militants, police personnel, Indian soldiers; whoever was brought to him. He did not ask any questions, nor did he show any reactions. If Shabir Shah and Yasin Malik had been brought to him, his face would have remained the same, impeccably impassive. In early spring of one of those years, on the night of Herath (Shivaratri), the doctor was dragged from his house and killed.

After the firing stopped, Gafar went into the street, closed Neelesh's eyes and wiped the blood from his face. Neelesh's glasses were shattered, only the frames remained. Gafar took them home. They are among the few last things that belonged to his sons, wrapped up in the scarf Amina wore when she was a bride. Gafar kept watch over his friend's body all night; he could not get anyone to take it to the hospital. In the morning, the soldiers cremated Dr. Safaya properly. A dozen or so gathered around the pyre. There would have been more, but fear kept them away.

A year later, when Amina was very ill, Gafar had a dream. Dr. Safaya said to him, "Gafar, take Amina to Ludhiyana. Here is a note for my friend, Dr. Mahendra Dhingra. He is a specialist; he will treat her and make arrangements for your stay." When Gafar woke up, he searched for the note in his bed. The dream was so vivid, but some of the details were shocking. Gafar noticed that Dr. Safaya's body had shrunk so that he looked like a dwarf.

He had lost one arm, and there was an open wound in his throat—one deep, protracted knife wound, not the multiple gunshot wounds in the head, chest, and abdomen. The blood around this hole in Dr. Safaya's throat had dried out. It was like the mouth of an ancient cave. There was blackness inside. ▣

A Country Without Borders

Poplar trees are like sentries guarding
Residences of powerful people
Important buildings, these days even
Mosques and temples! Still, vigilant
Forever like that.

Other trees, of differing shapes,
In somnolent darkness look like raging
Tigers coming out of their lair,
To attack the vicious supernatural
Beast slouching non-stop
Taking advantage of thick foliage.
The horse was dreaming of something
Nicer. He is not ready for more toil
At 2:00 AM.

Everyone knows there are two giants
Waging war with each other, while small
People deliver boxes of apples
To the nearby town, for export beyond
Borders. One has to be on guard
At checkpoints, lest someone assume
He is a militant and the boxes
Don't house apples. Yes, they have
To be on guard, twice over
Against militants who call themselves
Patriots; a country without borders
Would not need them.

A few kilometers beyond Kulgam
Past the dusty little exit to Amun,
Sounds of Veshav's mountainous flow

No longer reach them, in the wagon
A nine years old boy thinks stars are
Brighter worlds than the blighted one they
Inhabit, which he loves nevertheless,
For it houses a mother, a father
Sister, many smaller brothers and sisters

This country, the grown man driving
The wagon in the chill of a September night,
Thinks has too many borders on all sides,
Inside too: every few miles a check-post
Like hell's gate; then the den of others hiding
Behind buildings and trees, sometimes
Coming at you unawares.

The father, we surmise he is father, he could
Also be maternal uncle, sings a song
It is not the song of *azadi*.
It is the song of the mythical country without borders
Routes free for trade and travel
To export apples and silk, even milk and cheese.
Wedding parties on roads, dancing, drunk
Provoke chastisement for lewdness
From bejeweled, star-spangled mother of bride

A country without borders
Let my country be, the wagon diver
Stops by a small rivulet, washes his hands,
And prays, as the boy and horse dream.
Three thousand years ago, this was a country
Without borders, with no phone lines
For birds to hang on to, like watchful, vicious
Spies.

Thinking of Kashmir in Nanjing

Home to rare species of trees,
Ming tombs, rivers, lotus ponds
Snakes, toads and the turtle

Noise and silence; cars parked
On what should be unhampered
Side walks.

The Confucius temple, magic of lights
On a July night
Strange foods, wet, shiny streets
Made safe by some relic from the past
At entries, turning points
When suddenly a group of people
Men, women, children
Who you did not know walked
The night like you,
See you, greet you; make room
For you

Home is what is on people's faces
What you read; what they are
Willing to let you read: that which shows
Inadvertently—rise, and fall of a thought.
Home is not a flag, not history, not visa
Not passport; though in Nanjing
You were asked to carry copies of both
At all times, since there are police check
Points everywhere
Though people who man these posts
Don't wear police faces, only uniforms
Sagging on frail shoulders

Yes, Nanjing has had its history,
Some of it painful; yet, beyond that, and this,
Are people; born to die, suffer
Alone, or with others, be buried in tombs
Marked, or unmarked, stay absorbed
In their own thoughts

Time, so long gone, of streets
Though not identical to Nanjing,
Somewhat the same, here and there
Shop fronts, small bakeries
Owned by one man, or woman
The potato seller with only
Ten left in her basket at the end of a day
Fish markets, greens I have not seen
Since Kashmir—in Anantnag, Kulgam, Sopore,
Mattan, Devsar, Thajiwore, Bijbihara
Khannabal, Srinagar, Shopian, people absorbed
In weighing options, rise and fall of thought
Even in prisons and police stations.
Or, on a Sunday morning
Crossing bridges, driving wagons
Waiting for buses, negotiating
Bride price.

Dullness of life is not so dull, after all
Flow of water, movement of leaves
On a summer afternoon is intoxicating
Like the jug of wine, the book, and the Beloved
Not sensational like traffic accidents
Mass killings, arguments lost and won
About primaries and general
Elections, bets, lotteries; rise and fall of waves
Keeps time to light rain
No victory song; but birds regard it
With awe!

Winter Light

Leisure:
Dogs sleeping in the sun—sweat
And dust blotch his hands, his feet.

He would like someday
To write poetry, if there was money,
To make movies

Labor
At the construction site while thinking
Of Tolstoy, desire to have been a
Raskolnikov: to sin, seek salvation, to suffer

Blotches:
Is it possible to wash at the canal?
Go down the steps
When day's work is done; lamps are lit,
Women have put out the fires.

Lazy dogs
In Kashmir, Anantnag, to be more exact,
When he returned from school expecting
Mother at the street corner
They slept like this; he wanted to do something
Outrageous, hurtful, to wake them

He didn't.
Heard animals screaming
In the slaughterhouse, near the bus stand
Beside that hill where jackals roamed, crocuses
Bloomed, ghosts wore strange clothes.

Hell is murky
It is a terrible thing to have no light
Imagine tears falling like rain, not into the earth
To make flowers; salt burns into skin.

Letter from nowhere
From his mother's cousin
Beauty of winter trees and light
In some place very cold
Where dogs cannot sleep on the street.

And, yes there is heaven, after all
She says, "how can I say how ethereal
The light is"—when blue becomes
Some rare shade, in photos she sends
Captions like: *winter light is paradise*
Icicles make good sculpture

He did it: not really wanting to
A ghost wearing strange clothes
Breaks in, steps so close to his bed, speaking
Words in no language he can understand.

He will rise
Lift his spirits; know just how to hang his body
In the cell, let the milk-sugar tea stay calm
Form a line around the rim
Insects settle comfortably in the food tray.

Of sky, ocean, earth
That will be his sign, icicles catching
The sun; cardinal hopping on bare branch
Out of nowhere, dissolving into winter light.

My Father's Country

The moon un-reports deaths,
Absences; she shines tonight
Too, faint amid fog.
Embers blaze blue inside
Bakeries, as oil soaked hands
Mold hard dough into bread,
Paper-thin.

Heavy thumps, furtive knocks.
A gloved hand searches safety
Against troops, jeeps, whistles,
Sovereignty's relentlessness
Death rattle, two spent beasts
Growing new heads, when one
Is cut off.

Democracy is Andromache,
The virtuous wife whom
The weather beaten Greek ship
Leads away from home
To Achilles's son; who else could it be?
She will submit to his caresses
At night, as brave Hector's
Ashes grow very quiet, water of
Her tears all dried out.

She had to give away
Their first-born son, Astyanax
Only a child, to be hurled
From battlements
Of a city built by his ancestors,
Washed by the blood of his many
Uncles.

Only today, in the noon sun
The city square was drenched
Again in the virginal blood
Of Polyxena, Priam's daughter
She sang at festivals; from her
Chaste hands patron gods
Received oblations. She, whom
Achilles loved and whose sacrifice
His ghost demanded. That is how
Odysseus explained it.

It is the city where Astyanax
Opened his eyes many times
To blood curdling prophecies
By Cassandra, his other aunt,
Apollo's high priestess

The men who take him away
From Andromache's arms
Are kind; one says he'll prepare
Sandalwood, another promises
Flowers, washing of wounds in sacred
Waters.

The herald's voice cracks when he says he
Will knit the little body together
Somehow.
So the father will know his son
In the other world, lift him up
In his arms: kiss his brow.

My father's country is not ancient Troy
Just another place of force
Where weather darkened timber
Eves hide Ovid's red-breasted swallow.

A war bird rages and raves,
As a tongue less Philomela turns, once again,
Into a nightingale

She waits for roses to bloom
In the city's gardens;
What city? What lowered flags
Lie muffled in a heap?

Azadi: 1989-1995

In November rain
I look for you,
Shivering in a red coat,
Holding back words.
Dried flowers pressed inside
An old book, perfumed by
Whose trembling hand?

Last leaves on bare branches
Shudder to see me so young,
Peering at names of houses, numbers:
Not in any sequence.

I thought that you lived here,
Somewhere near *Sherbag*
Fenced with ivy, the ancient
Garden smells of death.
Rose beds are graves, fountains
Speak of tear-dried faces—
Their unaccounted for grief.

The streets near *Sherbag*
Used to be wider, sunnier.
Rows of ugly houses did not crowd
Like they do now.

Thirty years ago, four *Chinar*
Trees stood stout and solid
Inside the high walled garden
Of my school right around
The corner. We used to play a game.

Something to do with the distance
Between *Chinars*.
How we made triangles and crosses
Getting from one to the other.

Why are the shops painted green?
Graffiti on the walls tells
Me a bad story: a blackened tricolor.
Pakistan's banner installed in its place,
Its half moon being kissed
By suppliant lips!

In those days too people had a vision
Of the Land of the Pure;
Azadi was a cloud of fragrant smoke
It was intoxication of the *maikhana*
The celebrated drink-house, that
Reverberated with tinkle of glasses
Joy of the spirit; it was Rumi.

The police station was not a
Place of danger.
People sat around and talked
Of *Azadi*, as if she were
A woman in Persian legend,
Layla perhaps.
The Mujahid was no sly,
Self hating, masked killer, but
Majnu.

He who journeys
With the moon and the sun,
Wild wind and black clouds
When stars hide their faces

In a vast desert, and the desert
Runs ahead of him!

What nation
Does not have a dream like that?
History is a nightmare
From which we cannot wake:
We cannot arise.

I have heard of house to house
Searches for young men with beautiful
Hair who hide frightful weapons
In their sister's hope chests.

To the women who love them
They tell nothing except that
One day *Azadi* will arrive
At everyone's doorstep; life will become
Prettier, honorable, suddenly more
Pious.

Who are these men?
I would like to ask you.
I would like to know
Why their dream of *Azadi*
Excludes me, and my people.

Those who were born here,
But were not entirely free.
They did not dare to dream,
Whisper, or scream

You thought *Azadi*
Could be courted, wooed, and wed

Without shedding blood;
You thought it could be made to
Become a wife who does not stray
Never demands a price, or sacrifice.

The Yellow River

A cobbled street
Echoes my footfall.
Time dented stone
Faces, dust-dyed,
Worn by rain
And ice, frosts at midnight.

In dark, they listen
With lowered lids, carts
Coffined in black reach the yellow
River.

A mad man's song for tomorrow's
Dead, seeps through feathery
Quilts, into dreams about the dead.
Of graves, and caves that open
Doors to the roaming beast—
Sometimes he yields his prey
To others better than him at
Carnage.

In July, the river overflows
Its banks leaving behind mud
Mounds, washed white to paint eyes, lips, hands.
Slipping, staggering feet
Of those who died last week,
The week before,
Yellow river gluts, loses count
Loses memory.

Leaf shadows, silver
Shimmer fish,

A small cherry blossom wound,
Mute contusions, deep blue
And purple
Brave head that fell in
Ambush.

Father

It is you
Talking to me.
Who was in your
Nightmare?
When a midnight moon
Became so terrified
And you walked
Over to the kitchen
Made tea with milk.
You prayed.

You recalled
The blue and green van
Which stopped near our door.
Someone knocked
Three times.
You heard the van pull away.
Then, you wanted to check.

My head,
Limp, uncut hair, bloodied,
Fell out. My crushed hands
And shoulders you could
Not bear to see.

Tonight
I am home with you,
Sleeping
In a room downstairs:
Not my own room
Next to yours
You have boarded that up

With all my paintings
And love letters. I know.

Your soft step comes close,
It goes away till I can't hear.
In your own home, my father,
You cannot find the Door.
Within which is Mercy.
Outside is Death. I cannot rise!

Summer Rain

Rain in Wisconsin reminds
Me of rain in Kashmir,
When my mother was young.
She made a special kind of rice cake.

July rain was good for crops,
For fruit, and the wild grasses,
That grew behind our house
In an abandoned yard;
There were two weeping willows.

Their leaves, like fingers, brushed
Against amber skies at dawn;
At dusk, my mother lit an oil lamp.

Set it on a ledge near
The west window, praying
To the setting sun;
It is repentance, she said,
Not prayer. Penance
For what went wrong throughout
The day. Wrongs happen.

When it got dark
Mother removed the lamp
Put it in front of an image
Of a goddess, blue black.
Bloodied skulls
She wore for necklace.
Her flame red tongue: *Kali*
Goddess fierce.

July rain still falls in Kashmir
Gently like tears of a mother
Who is no goddess; who says her body is now a
Bundle of dry sticks
She will die in exile, be cremated in
Some strange place,
Holding on the last thought, as
Daughters deny her
Sons forget.

Anantnag

I took pride in your
Natural springs,
Your navigable river;
Every April we went
To Mattan, offered libations
To the dead: my father's dead,
My mother's dead.

No dead of my own then,
Life was eternal.
I could sense it when we
Gathered blue lotuses to
Lay at the gold plated
Doorstep, bronze sun disk:
Majestic, bedazzling.

Thirty years journeyed
Past us, leaving behind
Hoof taps on stone.
Spring and autumn skies grew old
Listening to night ragas
Un-chronicled silences of a very
Cold moon.

Apple trees you planted
In the backyard are tired
Of bearing fruit;
They no longer blossom
When cardinals announce
Change of seasons.

Their leaves look pensive
To the squirrel,
Hunting greedily for walnuts
She buried late last autumn.

The watchman, who opens the front-gate
Will close it fast in my face,
Without asking my name.
Still, my expatriate feet drag me back

To you, evening shadows stare at me
With blind eyes; cool breezes say:
Maybe, only may be, we knew you
Then; what of that? Now, you are a
Stranger: an Enemy.

Piles of garbage along
The hospital walls, broken bottles
Blood soaked bandages.
I want to say, *Look! My little sister*
Died in this hospital.
Her body was taken from here
To a house of mourning:
That is what I have come for.
Not to question *azadi*, or ask
My share.

Black curtains on windows tell me
To go where I came from.
Children stare with suspicion. They
Have learnt to hate; they are afraid.

Hollow-eyed ghosts
Walk the streets
Beneath a sorceress moon, muttering
Curses, adding up the dead;
The hill says no welcome to me
Still looks like a camel's back.
It *is* haunted.

Mother's Day

[For Kashmiri Mothers]

A fringe of leaves
Outside your window
Casts intricate shadows.
You sit up in bed:
It is only the wind.

You remember
Birth cries, the slime
Of womb waters,
Clean hair afterwards
Like sepals of tulips,

First taste of milk on soured
Lips, ephemeral, like sliced roses
Seen through glass.

Dream brush of lashes
Barely visible
Dimples on little feet,
Pale plums of summer,

Nails are so sharp already
Fists clench. Feet grow heavy,
Descend down the stairs;
Cave them in.

Year after year,
Caravans pass you by.
Without regret, gold dust
Settles on autumn leaves.

Your dream becomes
A distant house
You reach it, a shadow
Slips out the door,
Then another. A thousand
Shadows gather around
And you scream.

You have nothing more to
Say. Pursed lips
Watch refugee camp dereliction
With indifference; in Jammu,
Udhampur, Pathankot: your exile.

At home, in Kashmir,
You have learnt
To beat your breasts
Like a madwoman
To keep out the hunter;

Your milk too, my mother,
Has turned bad. The blood
Is still yours

To rage against, rage
My Lioness!
The fire of your womb
Is in trees, lakes and stone.

Mahtab

Mahtab was a virtual orphan
My mother took in. She put warm,
Clove scented oil
On the welts, blue and purple
Bruises.

She became Mahtab's intermediary
Sent her home unwillingly
One evening, the girl lost a spatula
Fine copper with silver polish;
Too good a thing to lose!

It was
Late November cold
Of Kashmir:
Knee deep in water,
The girl
With a dark face
Could not find
The spatula.

No one jumped in the river
To help her; everyone watched.

It was night already
And Mahtab lunged after
Silvery fish.

They slipped from her hands.
The spatula must have gotten

Stuck between
Heavy, moss covered stones,
So sickly green.

How could Mahtab go home?
Bhatanya Dedi, she said
To my mother, *they will kill me.*

Mahtab's tears were warm,
Her hands cold like ice;
It took many full buckets to
Wash away soot and grime
Till her hair became shiny
Ten times thicker, fluffier.

She became beautiful.
Fifteen years later,
My mother went back to
Mahtab's town
And wanted to see her.

The girl had died
In childbirth; there was no grave
They said.

If there was one,
No one could find it.
Bhatani, why
Do you care so much?
They said.

My mother is not
A politician, or a historian:
She is not sure whose

Country Kashmir is, or should be?
What the official Law should be
What the religion?
Except consideration for
Another's pain; nothing
Too impossible
This little, hand measure of
Benediction.

In her dreams
Kashmir is Mahtab
Whose grave
She cannot find.

Bride in Red

Like a water drop
Inside a flower,
The unsaid, un-given
Is held
Between rites
Of death and love.

Shame,
Misfortune,
Misery
Remain unknown to him
Whose name
Tangles with the night flower
Drawn in henna
On her gentle palm.

Death wore colors
Of her wedding dress;
Look how black it is now!
The lilacs and roses
On her cheek wilted, un-kissed
Unseen un-blest.

The groom no more than
A young boy; his mother
Strikes a blow; her grief is a demon
She blames the bride in red
Not those who bring on these
Wedding-party massacres: *kill fifty*
Scare five thousand and fifty.
It works.

Few years later, bring in a foreign
Observer, show demographics
Argue for a referendum.
Age of big words, words, words
No truck with the human
Particular. Habitat. Neighborhood.

When rain clouds gather over Doda
Hills, in the eye of the storm
She will see his face once
As she had once when a friend in the bazar
Told her it was *he.*

A flash of lightening will brighten her
Path, away from neighborhoods
Into the forest: her basket filled with fruit.

The Cedar Forest

Borders of the river came close to me
As the city receded;
Did anyone hear sound
Of furtive feet
Headed towards the seven-tailed
Cedar forest? It harbors an about-to-become extinct
Species of Kashmiri stag: the hangul

A red cloud, like something made from
Feathers of slaughtered akepa birds, hovers around me, as
I stumble on something. It is a doorstep of rotted wood
An embarrassed temple: filled with deity.

An earthen lamp in front of Shiva, the Beloved,
Starved flame braves it, against black wind.
Parvati's body is half-revealed
Like parts of the brain light up with thought
And feeling.

With slow steps, I enter the forest
Sensing birds I have never
Known, shrubs clinging to the last leaf.
There may be caterpillars, scorpions.
Sleepwalking mountain goat, the witch with
Strange toes.

This is the end of pain, someone says
A youthful image is reflected in waves
Where the Luna shines fretfully.
I feel like someone else, someone who is tired
Has lost sense of time, history and place.

In these woods, filled with bird song,
I've spent my days and nights.
When sun came out
Like fog, my doubt, fear, suspicion ended
It was the bluest of skies
You shall be heard, someone said.
The stag will be saved
Seven-tailed forest will become a beast:
Benevolence!

Seasons

Summer breezes
Part leaf-lips,
Dark green,
Bright green,
White sun, red sun:
Steel gray
Afternoons.
Agony, ecstasy
Of a mid-summer's
Redwood tree.

Moon monopolizes
Hypnotizes
Pale green domes
Of a mosque;
A girl in rose pink
Silk and lace,
Lit by a candle
Waits for
Her bridegroom.
He is to be taken
Away soon after, during
Morning prayers.

Tarquin's stride shall
Ravish
Still sad beauty
Of a bride,
When winds change,
War winds
Not trade winds.
Trees will be bare.

Redwoods
Flowerless
Gardens without
Bowers
Growing random grasses
Rank weeds
Water without sound,
Without a ripple,
A few last drops
Fall on red,
Red berries.

January snow
Is hardly new.
It wears a solemn
Grace, dry eyed,
Lays out a corpse,
Without his
Face.

Priya

White nights have leafy darkness:
Inscrutable like fate.
Pathways of her mind stay silent
Like streets during curfew hours;
Grief stricken avenues shriek
Become quiet.

Priya watches people cross a
Distant bridge, she cannot hear voices,
Only shadows pass of daughters, wives
Grandmothers in green, red and blue
Sarees.

Some wear black, or brick colored
Burkhas, white cotton, or forest green
Silk, holding hands of small children
Bring home fish and fruit; in the market
They haggled hard for fair price!

They are the living. She is in hell,
Watching a pageant that had
Place for her not so long ago;
She too had a home.

She is chained to stone.
In a nightmare words form
Lips are too dry to speak
They bleed her tongue red.

If Priya were to jump,
People will watch her fall

Wearing a white salwar
Her hair elongated eerily:
The cursed witch!

Someone will, no doubt
Go mad, screaming loud.
A crowd will gather
Near the mosque, where a fruit vendor
Arranges apricots, cherries, plums
In high rise pyramids.
She might shatter them.

Refugee

It is midnight,
A fellow passenger
Wakes me rudely.
I am already in Srinagar

My suitcase is blue
It looks purple.
Cars, tongas, people
Who came to
Take relatives home have
Left.

The courtyard
Of the tourist reception
Center is bordered
By rosebushes that have
Not been trimmed
In a long while, not watered.
Wild flowers grow along
Dank walls, light spills onto
Spider webs.

Screaming
Fury of a night train
Bearing a sweet name
Brought me from Delhi to
Jammu.
A dingy, low roofed
J&K bus, a morgue on wheels
Dumped me here.

This is my home.
No one can stay
Forever
In the valley of mid-summer
Pleasure; only I can.

A hindu woman
In yellow printed saree
Found dead underneath
A Chinar tree
Four kilometers from
The Tourist Reception Center.

Strawberries
Sown into silk
Blink
At police lights,
Clinging to hope.
A thin moon
Wrings her hands,
Leaning over
Broad leaves of a
Catalpa tree.

An earth gray
Body bag
Is flown quickly
To my pale faced
Husband
He alone can do the
Last rites,
Light a sacred fire for me.

My soul
Ah! My soul
Will not return
Apples
Almond blossoms are my
Bare shoulders,
Ripe cherries and peach
Blossoms.

An inky river is
My hair
My eyes, a soft black night
My face parts from the moon,
In blinding light I fall and
Rise.

The Promise

I.
My feet say they are tired
Pounding the concrete of foreign streets
Face looks back at me, bewildered
Like an animal who cannot tell the Vet
What it suffers from.

Heart is a mute sentry, rambling
Blind in streets; trees are here too
So is greenery, fall foliage, what then
Do you lack?

When present is sliced off from the past,
It is bone, even dogs will reject
I reject myself.

My father's old country lost to
Me, knows my malady, is relentless
In calling my name as mother did:
As aunts called my name
Summer afternoons, in late autumn
Preparing for a festival of lights.

Amid the bounty of a mid-western
Summer, the country where gods
Decided to become water, fire and tree
Not create.
Where mountain goats crossed borders
Without fear, geese could not tell
Where they were?

It tells me stories, one about
The pale, white robed Pundarika,
The ascetic hero of an old, old story is chaste
Like the waterfall, at Aharbal

Musing amid wooded hills
Pensive boulders of Himalaya
Meandering pathways bring me to it:
Unawares.

Sheltered by leaves of an Ashoka tree,
The waterfall has conquered sorrow
It makes my dream

Fall on its face like toddler of legend,
Wearing gold anklets.
Shapely lips, morning breezes stir them slightly, holding
Back a wave, immanence of torrential rain.

An unfinished thought gives
Pause to the blue jay, painted bunting
Is afraid of being made a cage bird.

Unafraid mallards step on sand, near the
Pettibone-park beach
Fathoms of the Mississippi:
Once Ojibwe Indians lived here
Their dance reverberates.

II.

Does my father's country
Promise safety to the banished native?
He is mid-summer guest where he
Should be host.

After three days, he boards
A dark blue van; it will take him back to
The refugee-camp.
His face blackened by a sorrow
That has no name. No legitimacy;
It is so like him.

Can someone tell this man: "Stay
Don't go." Pull out your keys
Open jammed locks of your house
In Vanpooh: river town in the south.

See if the squirrel
Your twelve years old used to feed
Has her place where it used to be.

If the burnt down temple near your
House can be mended enough to let a deity
Have his home again.

There is no promise
Shadow of an old, rotting
Birch tree, in my yard
Where afternoon spreads
Its golden wings, takes
Me far.

Sometimes the first rain cloud
In spring wakes me and I recall
Kalidasa's *Cloud Messenger,* line
By line; like prayer.

How do I address my rain cloud?
What message can I give?

What city can I ask the megh to visit?
Whom to find?

All those who wanted my return
Are dead, have fled, are scattered.
In our listless eyes now, no image rises
No face, no love pleases.
What use is repairing the paths; unweed
Gardens tainted by death.

City of Dread

I.

It is everywhere
In courtyards children play games:
Search, arrest, imprisonment
Being informants, dying and killing.
They say sociopaths lose
Sense of another's pain; it is sport.
If this is a play, who is the playwright
Who the actors?

In the City of Dread they still
Bake the same bread.
It is poisoned, the wine goblet
Or, a cup of peach blossom tea
Is not what it looks like!

Who is the betrayer?
Who will fight the duel?
Can it ever end; why would it
End?

A young girl drowned in Dal Lake.
Last Saturday. Crowned in weeds
Black thorns, lotus stems.
The body pointed a finger, not at
The police, army, militants, but
A mix of man, animal, tree
Who drags and drowns, without being
Asked.

II.

Narrow streets of the city are
The same. High walls

Guard ruins now, not houses,
Like before, they block sight of
Sun, sky, river, mountain.

She wishes to forget
A death in the afternoon
In the next house, hasty funeral
Women weeping, children
Inconsolable.

Mother said, "Don't look. Close
The window." That night she felt
A slate-black column
Walked towards her, like a robot
Took out an envelope   .
With an address on it written in pencil
He said, "give it to my Nimma."
Why was it so real?
Why was the address in pencil?
Not in blue ink, as is supposed?

Wakeful nights remember
Streets she hated for lack of light
Congestion, absence of Veshav's
Night song: river in the village.

Smell of food, and perfume, Kabir's
Tobacco shop always crowded
Smoke rising so you could not see faces.
Shoemaker's leather and rubber
Grain and sugar sacks also have smell
That settles like pressed down outrage.

She wants red dawn to come running
Meet her at the corner, near the milkman's
Shop. Become her mother!

Kashmir Today

It is bitter cold.
And I am sick at heart.
Who is there?
Soldiers stand guard.
One relieves the other,
Stepping on thin ice.
Army boots always
Scared him. He wore
Soft-soled shoes

Whenever
He went to Srinagar,
To visit his eldest son;
Wooden sandals
With cloth-straps
Adorned his beautiful feet
When home.

He is barefoot now,
Treads softly on ice,
It is like shattered
Glass, strewn on Mahatma
Gandhi's path when
He led the Salt March.

He is an apparition,
My grandfather
He is asking a question.
National Rifles men
At Anantnag's Lal Chowk
Do not know who he is.

He is Aftab Ram
Of Kulgam, a village
Medicine man whom
Everyone used to know.
Their show of violence
Scares him away.

He lurks in corners.
It is you, my father
He wishes to speak to
You. Go! visit his village
His house;
Lend ear to his story.

Believe it.
He is no ghost,
Not thin like air
His white robe
Is real.

No shadow warrior
In a Samurai film,
He has been violated.
A newspaper bearing
His name, Aftab,
Or, Srinagar Sun
Reports horrors he can
Not come to terms with.

A Muslim woman named
Khadija appeals
To the Party of God,
Asking for her
Disappeared husband.

She says: *I am your sister.*
What have you done to my
Husband? My two years old son
Misses his father.

Name is Abdul Hamid
Dar. Age, twenty-five,
Five foot seven, dark
Curly hair, fair complexion
He has a ring on his left forefinger
With A.H.D. and a prayer in
Arabic on the inside; what
Happened to him, please tell?

A Hindu man's father
Has died, has been killed
Drowned in Jhelum
Waters when he was seen
Praying to the morning sun
On Makar Sankranti

A Hindu man, Pandit Shiv Nath,
Appeals to the Party of
God's area commanders:
Permit me to cremate
My father. Please do
Not force me to bury him.
That won't do
I am Hindu. Won't you
Issue me a travel permit,
So I can to go to Haridwar,
Immerse my father's ashes in
The Ganges.

My grandfather reads,
Listens, shrugs
His shoulders, walks on;
He finds out Khadija's
Husband did not return.
Her son became a mute.

Sweet syllables
Of Kashmiri prattle:
Mauj, Mauj, myani Mouj,
Mother, mother, mother mine
Crashed against
An indifferent wall, as he
Fled in terror

She had been hanged,
Hands tied behind her back
He was brought in to see.

In Pandit Shiv Nath's
Courtyard snow roses
And stars shielded
A frail, work-worn body
All winter. Spring
Rotted it away.

Aftab Ram's shadow
Grows taller, thinner
It falls on blood-splattered
Walls, as he reads,
Listens.

He is a shrewd,
Unsentimental man.

He does not weep
He is Kashmir Today.
He'll wait, wait

For my father, my uncle
He will wait for me across
The river.

Sukeshi Has a Dream

I.
Sometime in 1995 Sukeshi
Had a dream, in telling and
Retellings it changed.

In the dream, one way or another,
Illegally occupied Hindu
Houses in Kashmir have
Not been burnt down, or otherwise
Destroyed.

They are just emptied.
The windows, doors are intact,
Locks on them
Slightly rusted, outer walls
Still bear imprints of foliage.

Flowers painted for weddings.
Names of brides and grooms;
A lot has washed out.

In the dream, Sukeshi
Feels she has
To look up all her kin
In Kashmir's
Two hundred tree lined
Hamlets.

The Umanagari house
Displays marigold garlands,
Red peppers in a string,

Tiny cookie like pieces
Of bitter melon, thinner slices of
Asian eggplant.

The strings hang on nails.
How they battle with
Winter winds, summer rain!

In the courtyard
She finds worn out bits of brocade, an
Old muslin saree torn to pieces,

Home-dyed many times, after
The original dye has
Worn off. Some Jigri, or some Bhabhi,
Or some Maami, or Masi of hers.

There were always so many
Suki could never remember names
Or, who is whose daughter-in-law?

They all had nice hair, beautiful
Bright eyes without make up.
Suki wonders what the original color
Of this saree might have been?

Who might have worn it?
Discarded it impatiently at night:
Be in loving arms.

II.
Sukeshi wanders alone
It does not scare her.
Seems right that she should
Make this journey.

See how things are?
This is her home; her uncles
Grandfathers, relations through
Marriages, blood ties.

It is Amavasya,
Perhaps, the month of Kartik
In the dark she can still see
The temple of goddess Uma
In the village where her father
Was born and raised.

The blue spring
With lotus stems
Undulating, free of care
Sure of themselves.

Suki remembers
The summer
When she was three.
Devi Uma had come to her.
It was too strange.
She told no one.
Devi had said nothing
Given her nothing,
Only smiled
Not the enigmatic Mona
Lisa smile; a definite
Goddess smile.

Its light made green silk
Greener, brightened
Decorative fringes of vesture
Her eyes, arms, weapons,
And peacock feathers.

A woman's tears
Over a sick child at the feet
No goddess can heal.

Who was that child?
Who was that woman?

That evening
Sukeshi went to the temple
Holding her grandfather's hand,
Offered a full blossomed lotus
With seedpods and petals.

Devi Uma's lips, eyebrows stirred
She thought, just a little bit.
Shadow of magnolia
Caught in morning breeze.

A cat that looks at you with
Yellow eyes, privy to some mystery
That she cannot tell.

Did the goddess
Have something to tell?

III.
In 1998
Sukeshi's dream changes;
She sees the madwoman,

Tara, who would get furious
Livid with rage, if she saw a child crying
She would scream, attack the
Unfortunate adult, male or female
Threaten to take it away.

Tara's long, twisted hair trails
With the wind; she is a thousand years
Old, bent low, moaning, face
Covered in mud and soot.

Detecting Sukeshi, Tara runs
Wildly through muddy streets,
Village after village,
Dirt roads bordered by bramble,
Small footbridges.

Vegetable gardens fenced
By mud walls, thorn-bush, ivy
Star jasmine.

Chinar, willow, popular
Apricot, walnut, tree after tree
Rivers, streams, canals, whirling
Waves going about their business
Why, they have no tales to tell?

Tara and Suki have now come
To a place of sorrow;
Long, deep wails rise from
Around a public courtyard
Where there is a mosque, an
Islamic school.

Moonlight makes silver palace of
Cobble stone, an octagonal spring,
Ten trees;
It is not clear where they are now:
Some village.

The weeping grows.
It is not like Tara's moaning
Not like keening when there is a
Proper death.

Mad anguish, low, quiet,
Relentless, throughout the night
Someone has watched
Another person being hacked
To death, someone they love.

A firstborn son is being shot
In front of his father, who
Is tied to a tree.

Tara is screaming, but no sound
Comes out of her mouth. She wants
To make *this* known; it is worse
Than children being made to cry.
In the old days, when she raged
In streets, cursed.

Now, it is different. There, a woman's
Husband is dragged out of his sickbed
Taken to prison
Without his glasses, his pills, her
Brother was shot in an alley
He is an informer.

IV.
Tara's eyelashes have become
Pine needles, her face bloodied
And trampled; she is now lying
On dusty ground, weeping

For everyone; even dogs are weeping
They no longer bark at her.
She gets up, walks faster; now she

Has reached a center, some village
In the Liddar valley: Sukeshi
Follows her closely.

Tara climbs on top of a hill.
From where she sees lights
Go on in every empty house.
The valley glimmers.

Houses of all sizes
And shapes have clustered
Together like a Las Vegas
Play-scape, lit at night.

No one draws a curtain,
Or shuts a window, or door.
No one asks a child to pick up
One last piece of laundry, from
The clothesline.

Light fills
Sukeshi's dream, and
It dissolves.

Autumn Rain

I.

Rice grains
Are yellow gold,
Autumn rain
Can do no harm.
It will wash off
Dust.
Sun will warm again
The sweet, hardened
Kernels.

Saffron flowers
Have been
Harvested, rain soaks
Dumb roots.
Hits hard
At stray seeds,
Waking memories,
Forgotten pain of
Creating, destroying.

I think
Of a house in Anantnag,
It's walls, hallways,
Doorknobs, window
Sills, latches, hinges, bricks
Are hallowed by time.
I want to buy it. I say
My mother looks at me
Questioning.

She is young.
Weaving a basket of bright
Gold hay, soaked in sprays
Of cold water,
She sticks dried marigold
Stems into tiny holes
And turns to me: *Do you*
Have the money?

Father walks in;
He too is young.
He wipes his shoes
With care:
"It is raining," he says
Ruefully.

II.

This is no house,
No mother, no father,
But time grown old:
Unmoving like stone, earth
Iron ore.
It was all water once.
An earthquake caused waters
To recede
Bring forth Himalayan tor
Ridges, roaring, laughing
Waterfalls of
Kaunsarnag, Aharbal.

They had no names then.
It was summer, hills
Were laden with foliage
And fruit, a verdant valley

Had waited
A billion, billion years
For the ardent eye
Of the Beloved:
Drowned in her own tears
She fasted and prayed for a
Rose-tipped dawn.

In her infancy
The valley prattled.
Her milk teeth
Were stolen by deer.
As a young woman
She was courted
By many kings, empires;
Motherhood brought joy.

Sorrow came later.
What she has to see
And hear makes her
Pray for a deluge.
The Beloved
Is a dead poet, whom
No one reads.
His eyes are dimmed
Mind is vacant.

Before we know it
Raw-red flood will drown
Crops, cover them with
Mud so thick
Cows and calves, taken to
High pastures in summer
Will drown.

Their stifled cries
Disappearing
Behind crashed branches
Of oak, pine, cedar,
Before death
Cuts off breath
Reddish brown of necks
With white lilies on them:
Speak of atrocities.

Brush will glut waters
Around footbridges
Sink them in the middle,
As water levels rise,
People watch
Held up in a trance.

Mud houses will crumble
Fast, their roofs of tree bark,
Sticky red soil, growing
Daisies and idle dandelion,
Children's cries, muffled underneath
One wool blanket, gray
With green borders,
Their feet stagger, words fail.
They are carried
Away by the current beyond
The playground.

Neptune's wrath will reign
For many, many years,
Till winds die, severed heads
Of white horses, witnesses
To this great crime, seen by no
Human eye.

Brown and white cows
Wonder-eyed deer, easy to startle
Forest fawn, sheets of Kashmir
Silk, lamb's wool shawls
Too damaged to tell a story.

It will take years
For the waters to clean up,
Become a mirror
To summer foliage, sensual, filled
With desire,
Proud autumn leaves
Months
For glacier heads
To rise
Near Panchatarani,
The destroyer god will become
Tranquil.
Mother goddess, having lost
All her limbs,
Shall be the beating heart
To live in Him
Make him shed new blue
Tears for a billion
Billion years.

The Story of Ganesha

Ancient mountain home
Of many snows,
Caves of ice, and the Yeti.
It was here,
The daughter of Himalaya
Turned away from mother
And father,
Put away her playthings

To win Shiva
With her service, her beauty
Could not do it.
Shiva's wrath burnt
The arrow like body of
Kama,
The god of love—
The young wife, could
Not endure, fell into the fire.

Scorched by the blue
Flame of Shiva's pitiless eye
They were phoenix
And the turtle dove.

Parvati,
The mountain born,
Sheared her hair,
Smeared ash
On her breasts, turned
Deaf ear to mother
And father.

In tapas, she wished
To burn all that clung
To the soul, made it heavy.

Shiva wore snakes
Around his neck
Slept next to half-burnt
Corpses in bone-strewn
Cremation grounds
By sacred rivers, amid whistling
Of the night wind
Pine, wild chestnut groves
Burnt out patches
Of blue grass: the eternal
Undying, forming intimacy
With what is born to die.
Shiva, the mendicant,
The one without home
And hearth, without food
Sometimes.

At the end of her penance,
He came to her.
First in disguise, to
Test.
She knew and he kissed.

She married him!
Bore Kartikeya of unparalleled
Beauty. He whom all women
Love, but none can have.

Parvati created another son.
All her own: mother's keeper.

He told stories
When vagrant father was
Nowhere to be seen
And, mother was sad.

Mostly, he watched the door
When she invited
Gandharva men, played
Water sports with them
Thinking only of Shiva;
Why he wandered
The earth, restless, suffering,
Alone and unkempt.

It happened so often that
Shiva came home
When he needed her, not when
She needed him.

One such afternoon,
He arrived, covered all over
In dust, grime, ashes.
His red eyes burnt with a great
Hunger of which
Little Ganesha could
Not have known, for he was
Not a father-born.

Himalaya's grandson
Blocked the door.
Hissed and pointed
A fist, and the beggar
Took out his knife.

A death cry reached where
There was music and incense.
Flowers turned red.
In silence, Girija's weeping
Settled in with a dark night.

He waited till dawn, hiding
Underneath a cherry tree;
Then he lunged the same knife
Into the pale-green body
Of a young elephant, adorned
With marigolds, lilacs
And amaranth braids.
Dressed for a festival, perhaps.

The severed head clung to
Ganesha's trunk
Became his own. Mother-born
Reconstructed by Father's
Wrath, new love, and he became
A scholar, a scribe:
A cheerful, merciful, loving god,
Born of a woman only.

Washer Woman

It is midday,
She beats white sheets
On stone, calves tighten
Feet are firmly settled
Around pebbles,
Moss around large stones is
Slippery.

She carries her load
On a horse drawn cart.
The sun disk lingers
A giant embryo that
Has not formed all its
Limbs.
A martyr's heart that
Has lost all its limbs.

Rhythmic sound
Motion of grinding
Worn out
Rock, broken brick
Mingles with echoes
Of sweet little bells
On the horse's neck,
As his sleek body
Plunges into night:

Hoof taps on a dirt road.
Edges of time hurt
The eye, hand; they stay
On tree tops

Alert to passing of ghosts
Their gathering
In the woods; the washerwoman
Will not be waylaid.

She knows what no one
Else knows. Not even the ghosts.
She knows dirt that is left
In clothes: blood, urine
Phlegm, excrement and vomit
Grass stains, turmeric stains, pepper
Sting, ink stains, where the signet ring
Was pressed.

She knows the astringency
Of soap; purity of ultramarine
Blue, neel, the final rinse that
Whitens like snow.

Her home is a small mud-hut
With one door, in the village
Where saffron grows.
She needs no one. She is time.

The Ever New Poet of Kashmir

Garden was silent.
An old woman, dressed
In a scarlet robe,
Gold earrings wearing down
Her ears; she sat on the
Green mound, in the shade of
Two birch trees.

She was quiet, like a picture.
One daughter-in-law brought
Peach blossom tea, the other came
Out, to look over miles of rice, laid
Out on straw mats to dry.

They looked at the poet's receding
Figure, that was all that happened
On an afternoon when clouds
Were white, sky was blue.

Time flattened its wings
Like a dead bird, crushed by
The king's horsemen;
They passed in the night to
Grand purpose.

Birch leaves fell like flowers
Covering the path for his tread.
Someday this memory
Will become one with blind oblivion
Of a city grated: turned to dust.

Phantoms will rise from
Woeful Vyeth, in long winter nights
Only they will remember
Who lost, who won, who was banished?

Followers of Abhinavagupta
In the hour of his death, they walked
With him to the densest
Part of the pine forest, where
Sun and moon trickle in narrow rays.
He sang of Shiva. One last song:

Terrors of Yama, the god of death
The pains he gives me, O Hara!
Yama's messengers beat me,
Torture me; they have no compassion
They love to cause pain; Remove them.
With Shivaya you live in my chitta; among
These trees, surrounded by birdsong
You dally with Uma, your beloved wife,
Wrest these torturers, these enemies from me.

Twelve hundred years and Yama
Is not defeated; shivaya too remains
Unvanquished: Aparajita, Anuttara.

Dirge

Newspapers are mortuaries
Fraternal blood
Turns black like the earth in
Spring.

One was killed, hijacking a
Delhi-Srinagar bound flight
Many years ago; his photo
Was not shown. What was he?

School friends knew, knew exact
Color of his eye, who gifted
The ring he wore
On his index finger, the amulet
With smooth, black, oily
String around his neck, the tattoo
In Arabic, on his left
Shoulder.

He looked at faces
Of passengers, seeing nothing
A bird shrieked
In his aunt's courtyard, where
He had once, accidentally, hit
His cousin with a small bit
Of stone, nothing but a scratch;
But Ashraf was beaten, starved
For two days. He refused the food
Mother sneaked in. She should
Have defended him!

The gun behind him
Has a silencer, it shoots seven bullets
Only one is needed
He is slender, tender of heart.

Before leaving home,
He kissed his mother's cheek
It was cold as never before.
Wife ran from the kitchen
Wiping a hand on her cinnamon
Colored pheran with white
Embroidery, turmeric stains he
Can see vividly, when
The bullets hit, one after
The other, sting of a malevolent
Honeybee in Shalimar garden
When he was eight.

The wife wanted to know if he
Will be home when the baby
Comes, at the end of Ramadan.
She said nothing else.

An aging father's sorrow has
Settled into the house, like
Wood smoke, the son turns up
In dreams, asking
For money, without telling what
He will do with it.
Admonishes his sister for
Staying out late at night.
Begs for mother's forgiveness;
Tells his wife a name to give
The baby.

She remembers
Not the name, but his breath
On her neck; breasts now
Heavy with milk
She weeps, though there is
No official news
No body; he used a false name

To give his life for a nation
That he did not know, a country
Not his own; that country
And that nation, if there was one,
Disowned him.

What is then to tell the
Earth, when digging a grave:
Mother, wife, sister, the baby, uncle
Deposits a thing or two of
His into the hole—plants an herb,
Quiet like him. *Why were
You ever born, my son!* That
Cry will not die; it is immortal.

Betrayed

My sisters run to meet you
At the gate; you are late.
The bride, sitting in a corner,
Waits for you, who has come
Bearing gifts.

The red shawl becomes you
Makes your eyes darker
Your mouth more like the
Rose, just about to bloom.

I don't know what my bride
Knows about you, what my sisters
And cousins have told her.
She wears your perfume.

I know it.
What dreams I have had,
Do you know?
Unlock my fist, to see how
Our lines converged, but could
Not meet.

I could have loved you
Been a faithful friend
Like Gabriel Oak to Bathsheba
Everdene. Maybe I did.
But the world is too real.

Your grandfather's ashes
Blackened by rain

Your father's old age grief
Mother's tears
Brother's fear, as they shot him.
I was there!

Across my ivy shadowed fence
You pass the night—
Mournful mother, wife, you,
Veiled by verdant hills
A snow mountain, streaked in
Blood of your kin, dust to dust
Ashes.

Can you count the
Wild daisies I weave into your hair
As yellow finned fish glimmer
Amber leaves fall.

I did not kill; even so blood
Dries up on my palm, hides
Lines of you and I converging
Not meeting.

I shall rise, in flames
Lift you as you fall
Your breast split open.

Your two years old dies
Near your feet
His father in another village
Killed two days ago. I was there!

Love

Scarlet blossom
Of sin
Fire strong
To the very end
Spring fever of
The earth
My soul
Come, be a god
Devour the sacrifice.

Vishnu
As woman,
Front pressed
To the wall
Face turned
Sideways
Stone flesh
Of sculpture: sensual.

Our love is
A cobweb; spider
Died.

The beggar child
Gobbles
Chocolate cake
He needs
Real food; can
You give?

Winter is
A hard season

Heartless,
Flowerless, darkness
Falls over the bridge
Cold wave kills
Without discrimination:
Man and dog.
Spring breeze
Says your name.
You have nothing to
Give. You've lost.

Winter Sun

Not the staying kind of warmth
Only luminosity
Illusion
Something in it contradicts
Fog, bitterness of icy winds:
Flowering light of gold
As if in a movie
Untimely thaw, puddles in which
Birds dip their beaks
Expecting insects, perhaps.

Hard to imagine
What birds surmise?
Do they believe, Spring
Has arrived?
Are they fooled enough to expect
Roses on the bush
I am not
Cheered by the sun, dark pall
Of night is only five hours
Away

It defrauds brightness
Catches verdigris
In its weavings—to show faults
On dusty stump of an antique lamp
Its stains, settled dirt, are impassive.
Tantalus's uncertain fate

Pushes me down into fog
Dense as smoke
Icy winds, dangerous pathways

Along narrow alleys, slippery, treacherous
But, then I think. I think the bad dream
Of life has sap.

A cardinal's flight from winter branch
How bright red makes a line
Promising smudges on pale white skin
Of Asiatic lily: binding contract of the earth.

Excavation

I.

Forlorn city of broken dreams, dirt roads un-trodden
Weeds have grown so thick snakes hide in them.
Yellow leaves settled on train-tracks are time's Lament.
How can they be ghosts? When no one heard roaring pain
Twenty fathoms below a red sea

I lost something here, at this very place, so long ago:
Sequestered in the earth I know it will still be there.
This morning, when workers were digging
I wanted to go and look, imagined them thinking:
Is she a spy? Whose side is she on?

Wiping off sweat, blue caps re-adjusted, they looked right
Through me, their wives, a little distance away, burn brush to make
Salty-pink tea, sesame bagels from a run down shop.
The baby cries inconsolably for no reason, tears bigger

Than sun and moon will drown earth in a sorrow that has no end
It'll raise ghosts from unmarked graves, from ashes at cremation grounds.
It could very well call up the power of demons once again.

II.

Why can I not walk over to the construction site?
Take this baby in my arms, wipe off
Its tears with soft silk of my sari, kiss the little forehead
Say: *I know why you are crying and why you cannot*
Be consoled.

Sing inaudibly— song of the golden thrush
Saffron flowers dreaming in starlight, a world
That is finished!

Poets and Sages

The world stretches like a dream
In which you weave words
And rhythms, in which you speak

Of Egdon heath, its ugliness
And beauty, its indifference to men
And women. It's soul that they lacked.

You, who saw *flood tide, face*
To face, while Crossing Brooklyn Ferry.
Thames was not the same for you,
Who felt death had undone so
Many.

You are souls on wheels of fire
There is no recompense, no benediction.
You are not God
Who loves: you are cruel, hard hearted
Without blinking lay it open on the
Dissecting table— is it true love?

Tell me should I begin to
Unroll what ancestral vaults
Hold, folds of paper and cloth
Scrolls eaten by moth
Tablets worn out, broken
Off at end rhyme: what should I
Leave out?

Did you wish to become
Immortal?
Without floating lights

Placed in earthen bowls—
In the river that fell

From heaven; was held in check
By matted locks of a silent, sullen
Never-born deity.

He swallowed poison, more
Is left in the cup.

You know what went into
That vat of poison, what it could do?
In your own ways you
Swallowed bits of it; you are like

Dadhichi, who defeated
The demon of draught, released
Water from captivity
So fields would not burn in the sun.

Some of you talk about Prometheus
Torments he suffered for
Stealing secret of fire from the gods.

You re-do the plan, it was
Done too badly, too badly even for
Basics.

The badness limits you
Gets people angry with you for telling
It as it is. You say we do nothing
But wash, spreading out sheets
Of silk, we don't fault the worm whose
Body was used to make it.
On the loom, someone fell asleep
The silk has snags, we stretch, so it
Becomes illumination.

The Yogi

I.

They say a yogi has
To wear ocher,
Matted locks. Walk barefoot
On Himalayan ice

An American teacher
Says this to a friend's child.
He comes home without
Having eaten his lunch.

The little face is drawn
He fingers his food,
Holding a tiny ginger cookie
In his hand, as his teacher

Holds chalk
He asks: "Is your father a yogi?"

I know,
He is thinking of a photo
My father
With saffron tilak on his
Forehead; what can I say?

A yogi should be the young
Man next door, with his iron
Strong muscle and golden
Hue.

He has become a mendicant,
A beggar in his own
Country: a joke for everyone.

Perhaps the child would
Like to know
A yogi can be a warrior,
A charioteer's son; the one who
Drove the chariot,
And the one who sat inside
Head on his bow
Petrified by fear, and love.

A yogi will know particle physics,
Decipher codes, do war and peace.
Read handwriting on the wall.

II.

The sea is shoreless, intransigent.
My ship is weather beaten, with
Rotten planks. Behind is a fortress
Of blinding dark
Columns of radioactive smoke
Rise in front.

I lack sleep.
The sleep of Tamas
Of destruction, before
My resurrection.

My Death

I.

It is Thursday
Afternoon, spring trees
Are trying to tell
Me something. What is it?

Time is a trickster,
Dressed in rags:
Blue, orange, sea green
Sheep shearing in
Bohemia.

Oily dust polishes, what
Might have been pockets;
They are empty.

A dead river is still a river
Children walk around it
In circles, straight lines
Not being able to
Wet their feet, as they would like.

Luna is mother
Makes greening buds look like
Flowers, calls out to end
Their play for the day, come home
Go to bed; dream.

II.

My life will endure,
Its oceanic solitudes, necessity
Of no longer having to love.

And the terror lurks close
Cuts through blinds like a vampire
Bounding towards me

Bandaged all over, masked, as
Night winds bend
With implacable force, necks

Arms, wrists of
Trees, making them squirm.
It wakes me right when a freight
Train passes miles away
Making the house shake; how old
Are the tracks?

My death will correct everything.
There will
Be no skin peeling
From my bones, no worms
Feeding upon me.

Not a relic, no remembrance
Of earthly love
Shall linger anywhere near me.

Let it be the light that falls
Between bulbs of Amaryllis, before they open.
A wayward breeze parts them
Red and white: bitter dream of the
Newly bereaved!

Figment

I.

A wraith among wraiths
I prize a baby's first
Birthday candle
Shaped into figure one.

Place it beside
An earthenware vase:
Dark Blue green
Lit by a split Luna.

Mournful strains
Of Rabindra Sangeet
Light up a face
Beyond forgetting.

A whispering night
Wind brushes against door
Knobs, buttresses:
Shadows of stained glass
Shapes, angles, figures
Hieroglyphs.

Gentle "yes" and "no"
Of those who choose death
Like Kadambari Devi, a
Poet hidden inside the mind
The poet.

Mighty Bhishma
Who could die when he
Thought time was right.

Jude, the Obscure
Became thin like paper
Bleached white, he asked for
Water; there was no one
He had loved too much.

Madri, the second wife who
Chose to ride the pyre
Of her exiled king, to give
Him honor.

Yudhishthira, Kunti's son
Madri's step-son; he knew
Dharma, walked with his dog
To heaven and hell.

II.
Cold rain in October
Conjures a mirage in
Halogen lights.

Rain falls like applause before
It is time, falls on actors'
Bodies, their dialogue
Unstopped, gesture undisturbed:
It is midnight
In Spring Green, Wisconsin
Laced ends of skirts and frill
Drink up.

Stone has
Such fire, vapors rise
Dry up the stage
Actors are specters of another time

They cast no shadows
Don't slip; don't fall.

What is my relation to this?
Where is my nation?
Why did I feel betrayed when leaves
Curled up early this year?

I wear forest green with an
"American Players Theatre" logo
It clashes with flora across the red fence
Crape myrtle, Sun rose, Yarrow,
Maltese cross.

I come down the hill
As if in a sleep, a figment
Put out the light; to bed
To bed! To bed! Good night
Sweet ladies.

Autumn-Song: Kartik Posh

I.
When leaves gather
In fiery red
Underneath wild cherry
And Chinar, I return to
These woods.

In mud-walled hamlets
Hearth fires blazed
Once; farmers' wives
Made afternoon tea.

They went
To the blue river,
Filled their pitchers at dusk.
Temple bells rang true
Trees listened; the
Vermillion flycatcher
Paused.

Each village
Had its own forest,
Meadow, garden, angel
And demon, sorcerer,
Priest, faith healer, talisman
Maker: dreams and sleep.

II.
How many years
Passed?
By my reckoning
It might be a hundred.

I am this country's ghost
Bound to return,
Gather food offerings
In late autumn weeks of
Remembrance.

Rice grains mingled
With bur marigold, mountain lily
Smoke rising
From oblations

Takes me back in time
To the Shivaratri evening
When I was seventeen.

Spring flowers had
Begun to show underneath
Disappearing snow.

I think I saw you.
The fire of stars in your eyes,
Hair like the wings of a brewer's
Blackbird.

With slivers of floating ice,
The river was cold
But you waded fearless
Far.

Fleck of light was the fleeing red finch
Caught in water-drops
On your lips, sad-still, about to
Say something. Not saying.

I knew your mother
In the village
Your wife, and child

You seemed not
Of this time, or that
Not from here.

III.

Another autumn rain
Fell on leaf-strewn pathways,
A war torn village, its burnt
Down houses, land mines

Where rice fields used to be.
I asked for death to
Sever the tie forever

My feet get caught
In hawthorn, blackthorn
Wild rose, hemlock
Alien thorns bleed my soles
And, I am Nothing.

My ashes made the thorn bush
Red. Forty days
And nights of fever
Delirium, cold sweat of
The End.
Love
Became flower—
Fire cannot burn it
Water cannot drench
Man cannot give
Hand cannot hold

Forest Dweller

DID ANY OF THE CHILDREN call today, were there any let-ters?" Of his brothers, only three are left. Sleep unravels a world folded inside an envelope. Last night it was the *shraddha* of somebody, perhaps great-grandfather.

Shyam said, "Govinda, recite the hymns again. I want to memorize."

He began, and right then he woke up. That same ghost-house, not this one. Why? The peach tree, almond tree, strawberry patch, wild berries, crab apples, and rice fields are behind the house. Kash-miri roses. Shyam died last February, in Delhi, when Govinda was hospitalized in Jammu.

His Russian student is in Jammu these days. She is working on *Ishvara-pratyabhijna* of Utpaladeva. He thought of telling her about the dream, about his brother, about a place far away, yet not so far away. Being Russian, she would understand.

Everything that is close has lost shape, color and rhythm. Among things that remain the same are the streets in a town from long ago –houses, public buildings, mosques, his kids growing up. His daughter, Mridu was the youngest. One Navreh (New Year), they went to Naagbal, and he held her hand. Flowers, fruit. Water. Sky. Air. Five temples and a *gurudwara*, an odd shaped hill formed a semi-circle around the compound. In spring, almond and peach trees were in bloom everywhere. He remembered Mridu's red frock. Little chappals. Her bright almond eyes, and what she said, "Papa, you are so much taller than me!" At this discovery, she laughed like no one had ever laughed before.

No peach and apple trees here, only three guava trees. The river is far from where they lived. Water is scarce. No shade tree like an old chinar. His brother-in-law is in the Muthi camp. He is blind. His brother and nephew had to flee from Kulgam. Her brother, in Devsar, Kashmir, died last year. A sister's son died in Haridwar. His body was brought home. Heat, dust and grief. The rains.

"Papa, you are so much taller than me!" Her little hand in his hand, their laughter at the steps outside of the Naagbal gate in Anantnag. Why could he not recite the hymns for Shyam in the dream last night? Words would not come. Mind is letting go. The heart refuses. It haunts and hovers. Cobwebs, dust, sand, mold, soot, rust, rot in the mangled garden. Rise again, plough and plant.

In a reverie, the snow mountain is all around him again. Such a slight man, dressed in white, looks sunken in the padding of his wicker chair, staring into nothing. The three guava trees have disappeared. A blue night spreads out in the courtyard. Mridu is there, in the same frock. He can see the light in her eyes.

She is in the middle, surrounded by six others. They slowly dance, round and round, a speck of bright red. They become taller, and reach the sky. They raise her up. Mridu's laughter turns into a whine, then terror, but she does not fall. She vanishes into the night sky. The child fell from a third floor window the morning after Janamashtami and died three days later in the Anantnag hospital. It was a house in what was then called Nazuk Mohalla in Anantnag. There was a stream in front of it, a bridge, a pathway.

If he repeats this to anyone in the family, they will say, "See nothing is wrong with your mind. You remember everything."

If so, why then, when Shambu's wedding was over, did he think the guests from Mandi, Chandigarh, Kanpur, Delhi, Indore were awaited and the main ceremony was some days later. He told no one about this, except to Anastasia. She had enjoyed the wedding, dressed in ornate sarees and salwar-kameez. She showed him the *mahendi*, still fresh on her palms. From this, he could infer that the wedding was over and his children and grandchildren had gone back to their places. He had no real memory of any of them having been there. Not a trace.

Why then, Mridu? Why those streets, and the courtyard? Why Naagbal? Anastasia pretends she has not seen the tears, and hands him a glass of water. It is she who makes him speak of things he has not forgotten. ◙

In Search of Lost Time

MEMORIES OF KASHMIR ASSAIL ME without the aid of a Proustian trigger, without something that can count as an equivalent of the famous madeleine dipped in tea. I may be watering a bed of marigolds, adding salt to a dish, feeling bored or distressed during faculty meetings when lost moments and places present themselves to my mind. Each recollection adds more to the original memory, what it might have been. Often, an event is cut off in the middle like when a fruit falls from a tree. All I have to do is to pick it up, maybe wipe it off a little. Is it raw? Is it ripe? Has it rotted? Is it taboo? Should I pick it up? Is it a lure?

I remember a bus trip with my mother when I was four. I was pleased that it was just the two of us. Hangalgund, a hilly hamlet then, was my grandmother's natal village. Anantnag was a lovely town with cobblestone streets, wide and narrow lanes, hot water springs, hospitals, schools, and colleges. We lived in Anantnag in a rented house. Hangalgund was on the way to a tourist resort, Koker-nag, famous for the Trout Fisheries.

In Hangalgund, the distance from the bus to Mama's house, my grandmother's brother, could not have been that long. But in my memory, this little trek assumed the proportions of an epic journey. My shoes had holes in them. The soles of thin, whitish rubber wore out so easily and let in a lot of dirt and sand that hurt my feet. The dirt road we trudged in silence was parched. It seemed as if there were miles and miles of it until we reached the steppe. Finally, my mother said, "Here we are! A little farther and we will be there." We could not have been that close because the murmur of voices from a house filled with wedding guests did not reach us.

From this point of elevation, we could see the rooftops. Some were tin roofs looking silvery in the sun. Most houses wore layers of tree bark held together by red soil where daisies blossomed in this season. I could see butterflies, their colors changing to something else in the bright sun as they hovered over blue, red, and yellow flowers. The rooftops were like gardens of paradise, with so many honeybees, bumble bees, and lovely birds. At some distance, away from the houses, where there were groves of poplar and chinar trees, hard winged crows and ravens circled, making a raucous noise.

My mother said that right behind the houses and the trees was a slaughterhouse. She said if I wished to see how many sheep and goats were going to be slaughtered for the biggest feast on the day after the bride is brought home, I could go with my uncle. My father was a vegetarian by choice; he changed his diet much later, in response to a health issue. My mother's and my grandmother's families, in general, were dedicated meat eaters. In our homes both types of food were cooked. Why my mother thought I would relish the sight of sheep being slaughtered and would like it enough to wake up early was beyond me.

My feet were wet and I imagined they were bleeding. No matter which foot I leaned on to relieve the pressure, the distance seemed unending. My eyes stung with forcibly blocked tears. To bring my mother's attention to me would not be good, it would halt our prog- ress, interrupt her thoughts. My mother was very beautiful, and when she was in deep thought, she looked even more beautiful. How much I wanted her to sense my distress on her own, lift me, hold me, and kiss me. As it was, mother did not scold me for walk- ing slowly nor did she pick me up. She more or less dragged me along, as an older sister who has things on her mind would drag along her younger sister.

There are photographs in my sister's rare collection. In one photo our mother is wearing a traditional Kashmiri dress. I am the cranky two year old with disheveled hair. Mother is very regal. There too, she is absorbed in her thoughts. My aunt is also in the photo. They had not yet learned to smile for photos. They rarely took photos, only when my cousins from Delhi, or my father's friends visited. Everyone is looking grim in these black and white photos as if the camera lens is the ultimate stranger. When I see news photos of a group of Kashmiris these days, where people are gathered around a corpse or a number of corpses, no one looks as grim, which is strange. They look natural. There is sadness, mourning, tears, anger, helplessness, but not those fierce frowns of my relatives.

With or without cameras, the mind keeps visual records. On the day of the bus trip, mother wore a purple and blue saree, a greenish border also of silk, thicker than the rest, a narrow line of embroidery on it. She held my hand very tightly and said, "You know, don't you. Today is *ghar naavay* (ritual cleaning of the house before a wedding). I want to be able to help prepare rice flour bread and *ve'r*." *Ve'r* is the yellowed rice mush of an exquisite taste eaten with rice flour *chappatis*. The chappatis were baked in heavy wrought iron baking pans, then puffed up over brightly lit charcoal.

The thought of fire and food was nice. I imagined watching the blue flames rising from the embers, a thin film of hot ash looking like delicate silver-work. Inside the belly of each oven, I could see the fire without smoke locked in at the deepest circle. Rows of ovens, newly molded were set up for feasts of all kinds: wedding feasts, funeral feasts. Spirals of smoke escaped from artful holes in brick walls, then blew in the direction of the wind, spreading all over the sky, over fig and apple trees, clothes drying on clotheslines in someone's backyard, until they finally settled on ageless stone fences.

My grandmother was already in the Hangalgund house, waiting for us. Her nephew, Niranjan, was getting married, the same Niranjan who recently died in a refugee camp in Udhampur. In Hangalgund, Niranjan worked as a mailman. His little farm consisted of a vegetable garden bordered by walnut, peach, and cherry trees, a mud fence covered with thorny bushes to keep out animals. Nearby was a trout fishpond, with a few water lilies circling its edges. They lived a life not of riches, but one of contentment and dignity. That was then. In the last decade much has changed. In unbearable heat in 1998, a refugee named Niranjan, referred to as a "migrant," or an internally displaced person (IDP) departed from this world. In his final sickness and fever, Niranjan thought of the cool breezes of devdar and chinar. His dying mind held fast to crimson dots appearing on ripening peaches on the tree in his village home. When his wife's hand tired of fanning, and she poured out a glass of water from the aluminum jar, he asked for the waters of Kokernag, the place where Himalyan ice melts to form a puddle, then flows out.

That afternoon so many years ago, when I walked with my mother to get to their house, Niranjan waited for us at the door. His wife-to-be was from the same village. Still, it would take four days of boisterous festivity to bring her to our house. It might have been because I pestered him, or for his own reasons, Niranjan made arrangements for me to be taken to the bride's house that same evening. She smiled at me, took me to her room, undid my old fashioned braids, combed my hair in a style, tied a red ribbon on top, and gave me a set of earrings and a bead necklace. In return, I told her our family secrets. I said one of my grandfather's brothers committed suicide. One of his cousins was locked up because she was mad. I also told her my father had fainting fits sometimes. I don't remember if I said anything that was either neutral or good.

Over the years, this bride, Bimla, had four children. She worked very hard to raise them, took care of the cows, the poultry, the vegetable garden, the trout fish pond, did the knitting and the sewing, and still looked lovely, cheerful, and bright-eyed. My mother's theory was that it was because her husband loved her to distraction. Now, with time, exile and adversity, what would her face look like? In that horrid, decrepit shack at the refugee camp, how I wished to see her husband as the young man of Hangalgund again, the uncle who told me the entire epic, *Ramayana*, before I was able read. To this day, his version, recited with a lot of humor, and new twists to plotlines, has stayed with me.

One thing I became sure of during the Hangalgund wedding was that Bimla had chosen her husband, though no one knew about it. The families thought they had arranged the whole thing, and the bride and the groom were the last to know. That is what was expected. That evening when only Bimla and I were in her room, with a kerosene lamp set on a low, rough-hewn stool near her bed, she showed me a lacquer box. It was on one of the cabinets high up near the ceiling. She had to stand on top of two huge suitcases to reach for it. It had a lock; the key tied to her tassel. I expected the box to be covered with dust, but it was shiny and there was a peacock sculpted on the top lid, with all its feathers and colors spread out. Bimla asked if I knew that the peacock is the national bird of India, as if that is why she had labored so hard to bring this box to light.

There was a huge pile of letters inside the peacock box, and dried flowers. Some trinkets, including a blue ribbon, and a silk hand-kerchief that Niranjan had bought one day when he took me out to the bazaar in Anantnag. In this magical box, Bimla hid the letter Niranjan sent through me that evening. After she put the letter in the safe box, counting the rest of them once again, holding each between her fingers artfully like one holds a flower before placing it on the head, or any other part of deity in a temple, she eyed me with a smug smile as if to say, "You are too little to understand these big mysteries."

Bimla did not give me a letter to take back to Niranjan. There were many guests in the house, how could she write? While she and I were in her room, rowdy children burst in on us many times, and she yelled and threw them out. Later that night, one of my cousins came to take me back. As we walked in the dark, we could hear wolves howling at some distance. My cousin said they were jackals, not wolves. I thought about all of the people who must have lived in Hangalgund from the beginning of time.

My grandmother told me once that when we look at some-thing —say a wall, a tree, a rock, a body of water, a sick dog—if we have a well formed thought, or feeling about it, it casts a shadow that clings forever to that object. So, there are secrets locked forever within the shadows that fall between trees, closed doors, half open windows, buttresses, bridges, cow sheds, and tree stumps. I was about to think of something, to lock it up forever in the shadows of Hangalgund, when my father greeted us. He had come searching for us, using a kerosene lamp like a searchlight to find me. I had become so quiet and invisible. Father picked me up in his arms, handing the lamp to my cousin who led the way. Perhaps I fell asleep right away. ◼

Enigma of Places

A MIDNIGHT EMAIL SAYS, "I am leaving for Delhi in three weeks. Don't you have any plans this year either?" The sender is Uma's friend, Sharmishtha, who lives in California. Uma grew up in Kashmir, so Delhi does not hold early memories for her. It is just the name of a faraway historic city at this time of the night, as she works late in her office. In her mind, she goes through places she can remember: Rajghat, the Jama Masjid, Red Fort, Birla Temple. The sprawling neighborhoods: Pamposh Colony, Greater Kailash, Rajouri Garden, Tilak Nagar. Buddha Park. Lady Shree Ram College. Delhi University.

THE FIRST TIME UMA WAS TO GO TO DELHI she was fourteen years old and her older sister was going to have her second baby. Uma was very excited, not only about her sister's new baby, but about living in Delhi for two months. After all the preparations and the anticipation, she ended up not going. She and her father had to wait, and wait, for the Banihal tunnel to open. Heavy snowfall and ice had blocked it. After a whole week of waiting, they returned to Kulgam. This was Uma's first serious disappointment in life.

For five days, Uma did not speak to any of her siblings. She only read. She did not prepare afternoon tea, nor did she sweep and clean the floors of the four bedrooms upstairs. She did not iron clothes either, nor did she have to help dig out the vegetables from dark holes in the kitchen garden where they were kept to stay fresh for the winter months. Usually, she liked doing this because it involved lighting a fire to melt the ice and snow on top, to open up these little "vege-graves" by pulling out protective layers of hay and leaves to find, snuggled in deep comfort, bluish purple carrots, radishes, turnips, kohlrabi and potatoes fresh, as if they were placed there only yesterday. According to what her sister said, vegetables in Delhi are not as tasty. Who cares about the taste of vegetables? She wanted to see places in Delhi.

In the present moment, so far away from that past, Uma walks home alone. It is a lovely winter night. Her kitchen smells nice because of the slow cooking food in the crockpot, and the bread that should have baked itself to perfection by next morning. She prepares a cup of tea. She has run out of milk. It cannot be like a cup of tea one would find in a small teashop in Delhi. She has little packets of nondairy creamer, but that was not going to do it. A reddish herb tea in a white cup, perhaps there are cranberries in it. The other day, Uma took a Pakistani student of hers to a restaurant and noticed how the girl added salt in her tea, not sugar. With a pang of joy she realized that this girl is from Pakistani Kashmir and is also used to the pink, milky salt tea. During her visit to Kashmir in 1988, she had brought along some chamomile tea. Her brother wanted to taste it, and when he took a sip, made a terrible face. He said, "It's like medicine. How can people drink this stuff?" Perhaps their favorite salt tea will receive similar reception from a palate not used to it.

UMA'S HOUSEHOLD HAS gone to bed already. She reads Sharmishtha's message again, and prints it out before returning home. It is a short message and nothing more can be read into it. Her mother lives there, in Pant Nagar. Her brothers live there. She has a life there, a home. Uma has no home anywhere, because their home was in Kashmir. It is two in the morning already. She too must go to bed. She turns off the lights one by one, makes a list of things to do tomorrow morning, and brushes her hair. Still the same hair, the same hands and lips; she is the same. Yet, she is not the same.

Each day, from the days of that summer, when she was in Hyder-abad where she first met Sharmishtha—or from that winter when she could not go to Delhi—is connected to the next day like a link. Yet, there are black holes. The links in the chain have weakened, and are broken. She and her brother have not exchanged letters in years; she has not spoken to him on the phone in nearly two years. Uma looks outside at the winter trees. A faint moon makes them look strangely beautiful. She remembers the afternoon when she visited the Salar Jung Museum. When she sat down, a young boy walked up to her, and said, "You sitting on this spot means you will come again to Hyderabad and visit this museum." It was a strange thing to say.

Everyone goes to bed early; they never hear the dull rumble of some freight train at this time every night. It shakes the build-ing like an earthquake. Their room is bare, perhaps too big for the futon bed, but its simplicity and humility is pleasing. She can't see them now, but above their heads are two Kangra school paintings. A winter moon shimmers through leafless branches of two walnut trees outside. Uma has a dream, of arriving in Delhi, without lug-gage, without a passport. She worries that she has brought no gifts for anyone. She has come empty handed, and she has to find a train to Jammu. She has no reservation. She tries to make sure that it is in fact Delhi, but she cannot. She tries to establish the fact that it is the Indira Gandhi International Airport, but she is not sure. Uma looks around for signs, but there is nothing there to reassure her. There are no announcements. No people. No baggage claim. No language to go by. She has to just believe that this is Delhi. What else can she do?

The scene changes. It is now a train taking her from Grand Cen-tral Station in New York to Stamford, Connecticut. It is not the express train; it is the slow commuter train that stops at many little stations. Although train tickets look different, trains are universal. Almost the same types of people ride them, be it in Tokyo, or Milan, or Delhi. The trees are nearly the same, as are the puddles, the winter weeds, burlap, and dingy skies in urban areas. Stamford is the final destina-tion of this train. For Uma, in the dream, it is not Stamford but Jammu that she intends to reach. In either case, she does not have to worry about missing her station. Jammu is also the last stop, a big station.

Her thoughts drift in and out of sleep. The dream fades away, and returns, picking up the pieces. She reaches the last leg of her journey: from Darien to Stamford. Uma gets off at Stamford, comes out of the Station, still thinking she has reached Jammu. She knows, somehow, that she can walk home. That Stamford cannot be Jammu, and Jammu cannot be Stamford does not occur to her. In Jammu, she couldn't walk all the way from the train station to Ban Talab. It is still dark, but she can see hints of red on the horizon, framed by blue black. She decides not to take a cab but walk the twenty some minutes to her apartment, since she has no luggage. She crosses over to Washington Boulevard and remembers the tunnel she has to cross, underneath an overpass. She had forgotten it. Should she just wait? The tunnel is considered dangerous. It is desolate and dark.

Uma decides to brave it, one step at a time. Or, walk very fast, just one big sweep. Either way, it is almost done; she can see the light. She takes a final plunge and falls over something that is like the body of a cow, or a human, she can't say which. It is lifeless, but she cannot get her feet out of it. It is covered in something like a rag (that means it is human). The rag unravels into strings and threads, like wires. She thinks it has a face, and the face is very bony. Even in the dream, she observes that it is like a scene in a horror movie. Yet, the terror is real, and it is close. It is a struggle that will never end. It will go on for an eternity. This thing becomes bigger, and lumpier, more and more shapeless as if what she thought were bones have dissolved into lose flesh. She is afraid she will sink into it like one might sink into mud, and suffocate to death. She speaks the fear words audibly this time. Someone wakes up, and holds her. The sleepy voice, though unknowing at the moment, is like a flower that has opened its petals but does not yet know the difference between light and dark, between blossoming and withering away. This other, terrifying thing of darkness, she must acknowledge. It is the enigma of having lived in too many places and not being able to call any place home. It is the enigma of having loved the places, despite not fully being there. It makes one's mind a country without borders. That is her residence for now. If someday the mind chooses to go away, then, of course, there will only be this thing of darkness, this lumpy matter she encountered coming out of the tunnel. That will be an end. ◙

GLOSSARY

Abhinvagupta. Renowned Kashmiri philosopher and aesthetician from Kashmir of the tenth century C.E.

Aftab. Arabic word for sun, first name of a person, often male.

Aharbal. A hill station and a waterfall in the Kulgam district, on the river Veshav.

Amavasya. Day of the dark moon in the lunar calendar.

Anantnag. A city in Kashmir. Its name, derived from Sanskrit, means the city of many (infinite) springs. The term "nag" in Sanskrit and Kashmiri is the word for spring. Some of the springs in this city are hot water sulfur springs.

Andromache. The Trojan heroine is Hector's wife, known for her virtue. She suffered atrocities during the war, such as Hector's death, her son's murder and being taken away to Greece as spoils of the war.

Anuttara. A female, Hindu name, "Anuttara" means unparalleled or a quality beyond which there is nothing. It is associated with a type of yoga, and mystical power in Kashmir Shaivism.

Apparajita. A Sanskrit word that means unvanquished, and the first name of a female.

Ashmuj, Formerly a village, it is now a small town in Kashmir.

Ashoka Tree. A name for two types of trees. *Shoka* in Sanskrit means "sorrow" or "grief." When the prefix "a" is added, it means "without sorrow." It is also the name of the renowned king, Ashoka (304 to 232 BCE), of the Mauryan empire. Ashoka converted to Buddhism and took up *ahimsa*, non-violence, demilitarizing his kingdom after the destructive battle of Kalinga.

Astyanax. A character from the Greek playwright Euripides' tragedy, *Trojan Women*. Astyanax was Hector and Andromache's son, who was killed at Odysseus' orders at the end of the battle between the Greeks and the Trojans. One of the bitterest trials Andromache had to face was to give him up to the guards.

Azadi. An Urdu word that means freedom.

Banihal. A town connecting the Kashmir valley with India. In Kashmiri "banihal" means blizzard.

Bathsheba Everdene. The heroine of Thomas Hardy's *Far From the Madding Crowd.*

Bhabhi. An Urdu, Hindi, and Kashmiri kinship term, which means sister-in-law, and was also used in the old Kashmir for mother and aunt.

Bhatani. In Kashmiri means a female Hindu.

Bhatnya Dedi. A respectful address for a Hindu matron.

Bhatta. In Kashmiri means a Hindu man.

Bhishma. In the Great War, narrated in the Sanskrit epic, Mahabharata, the opposite sides in the battle were fraternal cousins, and Bhishma was a granduncle to both. He chose to fight on the side of

Kauravas, against the Pandavas. Conflicts between India and Pakistan are sometimes seen in South Asia as fights between cousins, with granduncles placed in a difficult position.

Bijbihara. One of the major towns in South Kashmir, in the Anantnag district.

Burkha. An outer garment that covers the whole body, worn by women in Kashmir, Afghanistan and other places in Central and South Asia.

Cassandra. A Greek mythological prophet, Priam's daughter and Apollo's priestess forced to go with Agamemnon after the destruction of Troy. Cassandra has the gift of prophecy but due to a curse her prophesies are never believed.

Chandigarh. A major city in northern India. Chandi is one of the names of the Hindu goddess, *Kali*.

Chinar. A Persian maple or shade tree, the leaves of which turn amber in autumn. Its dry leaves are used for fuel.

Chitta. A Sanskrit word for the mind, or consciousness.

Dadhichi. A central character in Indic mythology, devotee of Shiva, defeats Vritra, the personification of drought, and is credited with the release of water for the use of humans (held back by drought).

Devdar. A type of cedar tree widely found in Kashmir.

Dharma. Ethics, or ethical code of conduct as stipulated in Hinduism.

Doda. A town in the Jammu region of Jammu and Kashmir.

Gabriel Oak. A character in Thomas Hardy's novel, *Far From the Madding Crowd.*

Gandharvas. A name for celestial beings in Hinduism, who are skilled in dancing and singing. The term is sometimes used for musicians and dancers.

Ganesha. The elephant headed god in the Hindu pantheon.

Girija. One of the names for Parvati, the Hindu goddess of fertility, love and devotion. *Giri* in Sanskrit means mountain, and *girija* means born of a mountain.

Gurudwara. A Sikh temple.

Hangalgund. Formerly a pristine village, now one of the major towns in the Anantnag district of Kashmir.

Hangul. A Kashmiri stag that is a subspecies of the elk.

Haridwar. A district in Uttarakhand in northern India that is a place of pilgrimage for Hindus. Traditionally, Haridwar has played a significant part in post-funeral rites as the place where the ashes of the dead are immersed.

Hector. Son of Priam, the king of Troy, killed in the war between the Greeks and the Trojans.

Herath. Kashmiri name for the Shivaratri festival.

Hyderabad. The capital of the Indian state of Telangana.

Jammu. The largest city in the Jammu part of the Jammu and Kashmir state, it serves as the state's winter capital.

Janmashtami. Also known as Krishna Janmashtami, it is an annual celebration of the birth of the Hindu deity Krishna, an avatar of Vishnu. Krishna is one of the most widely worshiped and popular of all Hindu deities.

Jigri. An endearing term for aunt, mother or elder sister in Kashmiri.

Jude. The male protagonist of Thomas Hardy's *Jude the Obscure.*

Kadambari. A novel by Bhanabhatta, a seventh century Sanskrit poet and prose writer of India.

Kama. The god of love in the Indic lore, with arrows and all, similar to Cupid.

Kangra School. Pictorial art that originated in Himachel Predesh, a hilly northern province in India.

Kanpur. A major city in Uttar Pradesh province in north India.

Kartik. A name of a month in autumn in the Kashmiri calendar.

Kartikeya. Son of Shiva and Parvati.

Kaunsarnag. A mountain lake in the Kulgam district of Kashmir.

Kokernag. A town in the Anantnag district of Kashmir that is a tourist resort.

Kulgam. A town and district as well as the district headquarter in south Kashmir.

Kunti. The wife of Pandu, a king from the Kuru dynasty, mother of three of the Pandava brothers, including Yudhishthira and Arjuna. She is an important character in the great epic, *Mahabharata*.

Liddar Valley. A valley surrounding the Liddar River in Kashmir.

Ludhiyana. A city in the Punjab state in north India.

Maami. Hindi and Kashmiri kinship term for mother's brother's wife.

Madri. The wife of Pandu, a character in the epic *Mahabharata*.

Mahtab. It means "the moon." It can also be the name of a female.

Maikhana. A pub or drink house.

Makar Sankranti. A Hindu festival held in mid-January, conflated with winter solstice.

Mandi. A busy market town in the hilly province of Himachel Pradesh in north India.

Martand. A town near Anantnag, in Kashmir, which boasts of ancient ruins. Also the name of a famous sun temple.

Megh. Sanskrit word for cloud, as in the classical poet Kalidasa's lyrical epic titled *Meghaduta: The Cloud Messenger*.

Nagbal. A large courtyard, situated at the bottom of a hill that houses a cluster of springs in Anantnag, where there are a number of Hindu temples, a Sikh Gurudwara, gardens, bathhouses for women, shops, a temple compound, and community center.

Nanjing. A historic city in China, traditionally called the South Capital.

Navreh. New Year's day in the Kashmiri calendar is in March, not in January.

Nishat. One of the Mughal gardens in Srinagar.

Panchatarani. A river formed of five streams, on the way to the Amarnath cave, where an ice formation in the shape of the Shivalinga is reverenced.

Parvati. One of the names of Shiva's wife, a female deity also known as mother goddess.

Pathankot. A city in the Indian state of Punjab.

Pheran. A loose fitting gown in different styles, worn by men and women in Kashmir.

Posh. Means flower in Kashmiri.

Priam. King of Troy.

Pundarika. The male protagonist and the hero in the prose romance, *Kadambari* by Banabhatta, a seventh century Sanskrit writer known for his nature descriptions and long sentences.

Rabindra Sangeet. A musical style founded and popularized by Rabindranath Tagore, a Bengali writer of the twentieth century, and a Nobel laureate.

Ramayana. The story of *Rama*; one of the two major Indian (Sanskrit) epics.

Salar Jung Museum. An art museum in Hyderabad, in Telangana, South India.

Salwar. Loose fitting pants worn with a tunic; common dress for women in South Asia.

Shalimar. One of the Mughal gardens in Srinagar, Kashmir.

Sherbag. A garden styled on Mughal gardens, in Anantnag.

Shiva. One of the gods of the Hindi Trinity, patron god of Kashmiri Hindus.

Shivaya. In Abhinavagupta's hymn to Shiva, also means Shiva's grace.

Shopian. One of the districts of Jammu and Kashmir state, in the Kashmir valley.

Shraddha. In Hinduism, a rite for forebears who have died.

Soortrag. The word "soor" in Kashmiri means ashes; "trag" means a pond.

Tamas. The modality of lethargy, sleep and darkness according to Indic metaphysical theories of mind and consciousness. The other two modalities are *sattva*, which signifies truth, calm and light; and *rajas*, which reflects energy, passion and a state of arousal.

Tapas. A Sanskrit word for disciplined meditation or penance.

Tarquin. A king associated with tyranny in ancient Rome.

Thajiwore. A town situated near Bijbehara in South Kashmir, known for an old Shiva temple and pilgrimage that coincides with the more arduous Amarnath pilgrimage.

Tilak. A spot of saffron paste on the forehead, traditionally marked someone as Hindu.

Udhampur. The second largest city in the Jammu part of the Jammu and Kashmir state.

Uma. Another name for the goddess Parvati, daughter of Himalaya, wife of Shiva.

Vanpooh. A town in South Kashmir

Vitasta. The Sanskrit name for the river Jhelum that flows through many towns and cities of Kashmir. Vitasta is mentioned in the *Rigveda*; the Greek name is Hydaspes.

Vyeth. The Kashmiri name for Jhelum or Vitasta.

Yama. The Hindu god of death.

Yudhishhira. One of the Pandava brothers, the eldest, son of Kunti, known for his knowledge of dharma, one of the main characters in the epic, *Mahabharata*.

Zahar. Kashmiri word for poison. ▣

ABOUT THE POET

L ALITA PANDIT HOGAN is a professor in the Department of English at the University of Wisconsin at La Crosse, and Affiliate faculty of the South Asia Center at the University of Wisconsin-Madison. She is the co-editor and contributing author of three scholarly books: *Criticism and Lacan: Essays and Dialogue on Language, Structure, and the Unconscious* (University of Georgia Press, 1990); *Literary India: Comparative Studies in Aesthetics, Colonialism, and Culture* (SUNY Press, 1995); and *Rabindranath Tagore: Universality*

and Tradition (Fairleigh Dickinson University Press, 2002). She has also co-edited three special issues of journals: *Comparative Poetics: Non-Western Traditions in Literary Theory* (*College Literature,* 1996); *Cognitive Shakespeare: Criticism and Theory in the Age of Neuroscience* (*College Literature,* 2006); and "Hindi Cinema" (*Projections: A Journal of Movies and Mind,* 2009), and has authored many articles and book chapters on Shakespeare, Rabindranath Tagore, Cognitive Approaches to Literature, Emotion Studies, Indian Literature, Indian Cinema and Comparative Aesthetics. She has also published poetry and fiction online and in print outlets in English, as well as in Hindi. Hogan is a member of the editorial board of Ohio State University Press' special series on Cognitive Approaches to Culture. At the University of Wisconsin-La Crosse, she teaches courses on Shakespeare, Emotion and Literature, Critical Theory, International Studies in Literature. In 2012, Hogan won the University of Wisconsin System's Outstanding Woman of Color Award, and in 2009, the University of Wisconsin College of Liberal Studies Excellence in Research and Creative Endeavors Award. 回

OTHER BOOKS BY 2LEAF PRESS

2LEAF PRESS challenges the status quo by publishing alternative fiction, non-fiction, poetry and bilingual works by activists, academics, poets and authors dedicated to diversity and social justice with scholarship that is accessible to the general public. 2LEAF PRESS produces high quality and beautifully produced hardcover, paperback and ebook formats through our series: *2LP Explorations in Diversity, 2LP University Books, 2LP Classics, 2LP Translations, Nuyorican World Series,* and *2LP Current Affairs, Culture & Politics.* Below is a selection of 2LEAF PRESS' published titles.

2LP EXPLORATIONS IN DIVERSITY
Substance of Fire: Gender and Race in the College Classroom
by Claire Millikin
Foreword by R. Joseph Rodríguez, Afterword by Richard Delgado
Contributed material by Riley Blanks, Blake Calhoun, Rox Trujillo

Black Lives Have Always Mattered
A Collection of Essays, Poems, and Personal Narratives
Edited by Abiodun Oyewole

The Beiging of America:
Personal Narratives about Being Mixed Race in the 21st Century
Edited by Cathy J. Schlund-Vials, Sean Frederick Forbes, Tara Betts
with an Afterword by Heidi Durrow

What Does it Mean to be White in America?
Breaking the White Code of Silence, A Collection of Personal Narratives
Edited by Gabrielle David and Sean Frederick Forbes
Introduction by Debby Irving and Afterword by Tara Betts

2LP UNIVERSITY BOOKS
Designs of Blackness, Mappings in the Literature and
Culture of African Americans
A. Robert Lee
20TH ANNIVERSARY EXPANDED EDITION

2LP CLASSICS
Adventures in Black and White
Edited and with a critical introduction by Tara Betts
by Philippa Duke Schuyler

Monsters: Mary Shelley's Frankenstein and Mathilda
by Mary Shelley, edited by Claire Millikin Raymond

2LP TRANSLATIONS
Birds on the Kiswar Tree
by Odi Gonzales, Translated by Lynn Levin
Bilingual: English/Spanish

Incessant Beauty, A Bilingual Anthology
by Ana Rossetti, Edited and Translated by Carmela Ferradáns
Bilingual: English/Spanish

NUYORICAN WORLD SERIES
Our Nuyorican Thing, The Birth of a Self-Made Identity
by Samuel Carrion Diaz, with an Introduction by Urayoán Noel
Bilingual: English/Spanish

Hey Yo! Yo Soy!, 40 Years of Nuyorican Street Poetry,
The Collected Works of Jesús Papoleto Meléndez
Bilingual: English/Spanish

LITERARY NONFICTION
No Vacancy; Homeless Women in Paradise
by Michael Reid

The Beauty of Being, A Collection of Fables, Short Stories & Essays
by Abiodun Oyewole

WHEREABOUTS: Stepping Out of Place,
An Outside in Literary & Travel Magazine Anthology
Edited by Brandi Dawn Henderson

PLAYS
Rivers of Women, The Play
by Shirley Bradley LeFlore, with photographs by Michael J. Bracey

AUTOBIOGRAPHIES/MEMOIRS/BIOGRAPHIES
Trailblazers, Black Women Who Helped Make America Great
American Firsts/American Icons
by Gabrielle David

Mother of Orphans
The True and Curious Story of Irish Alice, A Colored Man's Widow
by Dedria Humphries Barker

Strength of Soul
by Naomi Raquel Enright

Dream of the Water Children:
Memory and Mourning in the Black Pacific
by Fredrick D. Kakinami Cloyd
Foreword by Velina Hasu Houston, Introduction by Gerald Horne
Edited by Karen Chau

The Fourth Moment: Journeys from the Known to the Unknown, A Memoir
by Carole J. Garrison, Introduction by Sarah Willis

POETRY
PAPOLÍTICO, Poems of a Political Persuasion
by Jesús Papoleto Meléndez
with an Introduction by Joel Kovel and DeeDee Halleck

Critics of Mystery Marvel, Collected Poems
by Youssef Alaoui, with an Introduction by Laila Halaby

shrimp
by jason vasser-elong, with an Introduction by Michael Castro
The Revlon Slough, New and Selected Poems
by Ray DiZazzo, with an Introduction by Claire Millikin

Written Eye: Visuals/Verse
by A. Robert Lee

A Country Without Borders: Poems and Stories of Kashmir
by Lalita Pandit Hogan, with an Introduction by Frederick Luis Aldama

Branches of the Tree of Life
The Collected Poems of Abiodun Oyewole 1969-2013
by Abiodun Oyewole, edited by Gabrielle David
with an Introduction by Betty J. Dopson

2Leaf Press is an imprint owned and operated by the Intercultural Alliance of
Artists & Scholars, Inc. (IAAS), a NY-based nonprofit organization that pub-
lishes and promotes multicultural literature.

NEW YORK
www.2leafpress.org